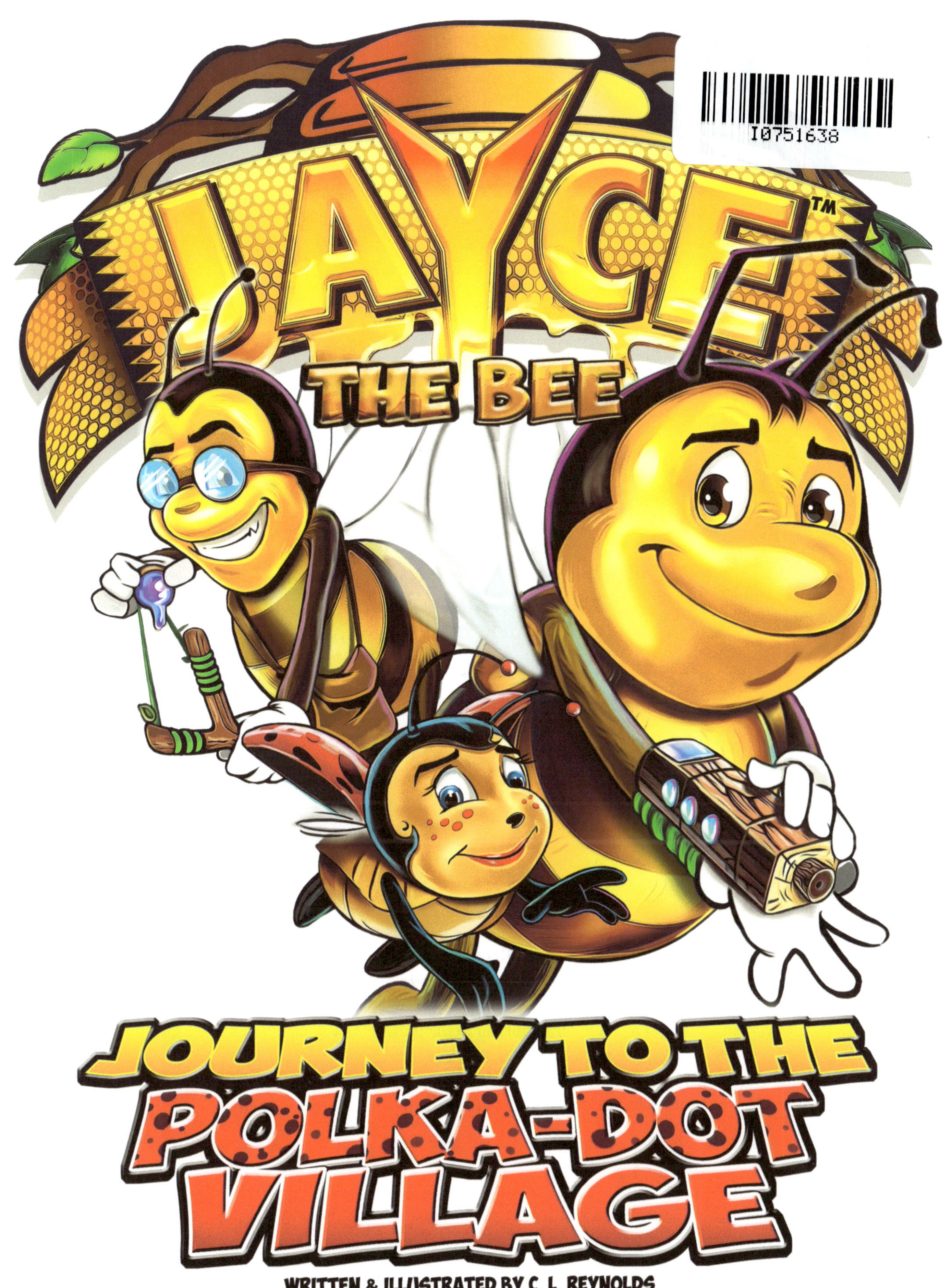

WRITTEN & ILLUSTRATED BY C. L. REYNOLDS

Book design and cover by Calvin Reynolds

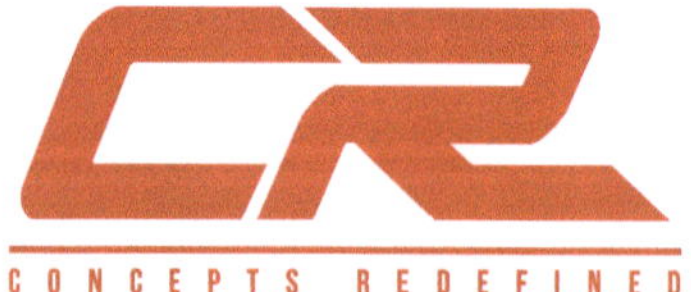

Published in 2017 by Concepts Redefined, an imprint of Calvin Reynolds

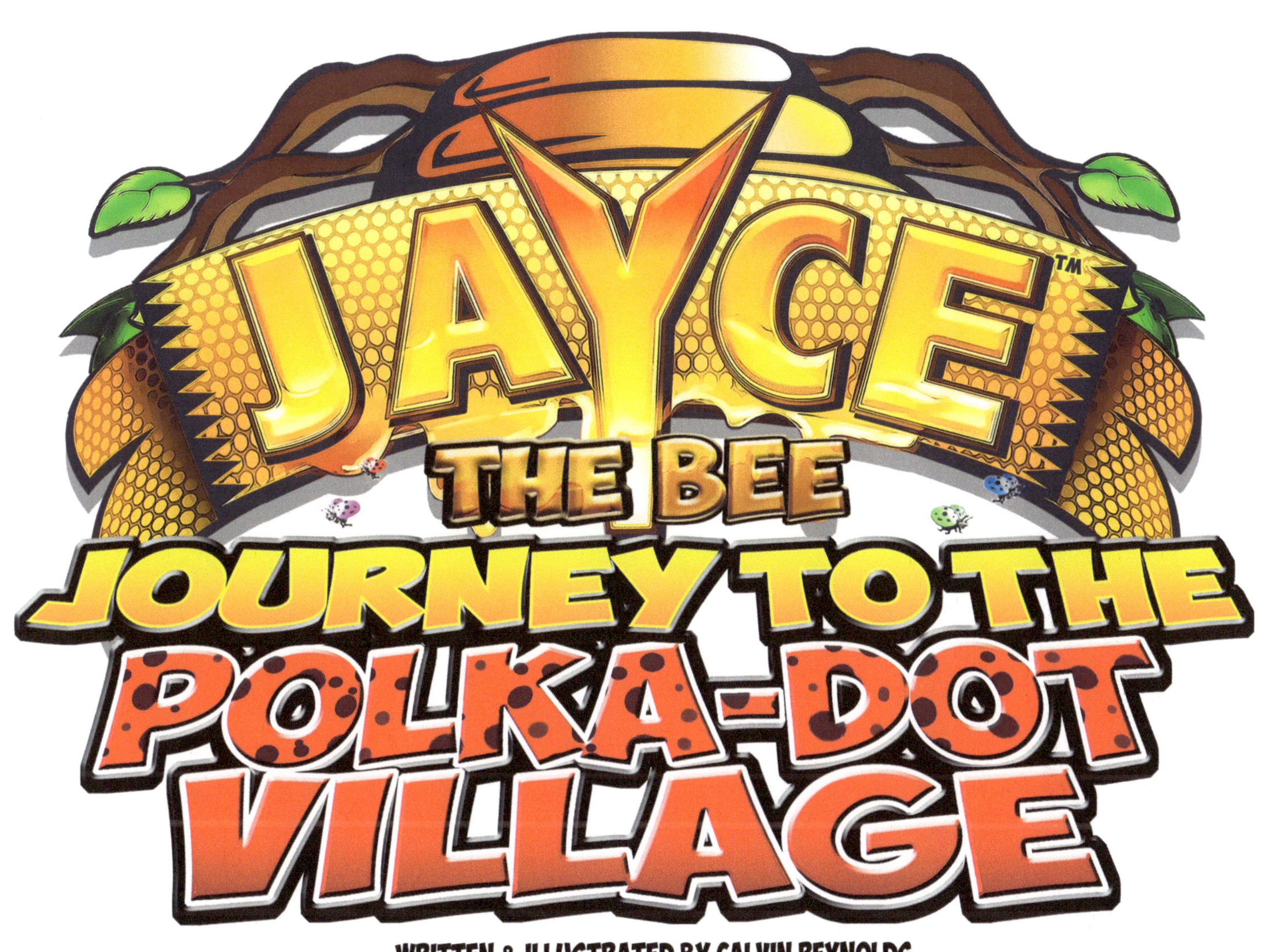

WRITTEN & ILLUSTRATED BY CALVIN REYNOLDS

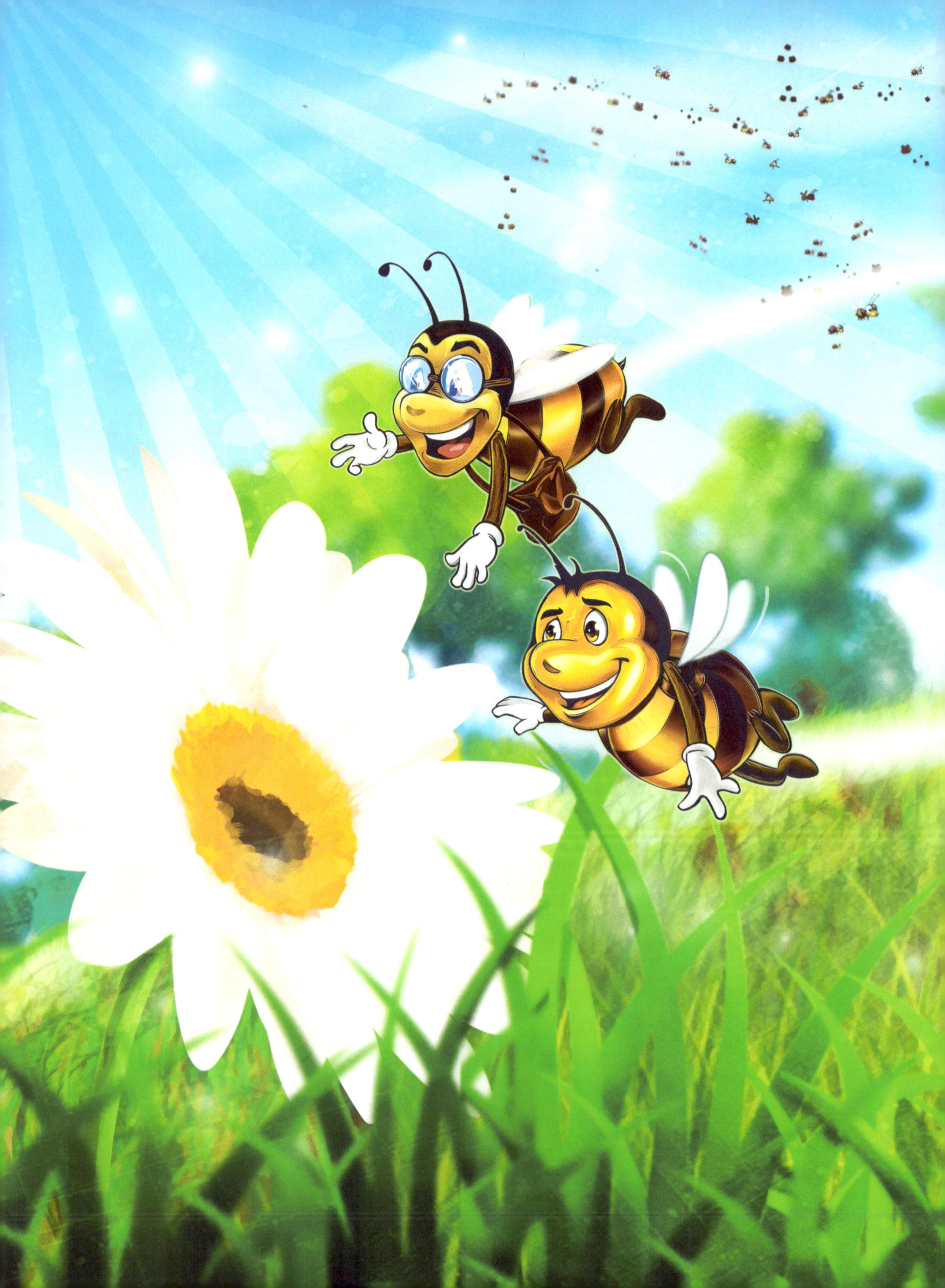

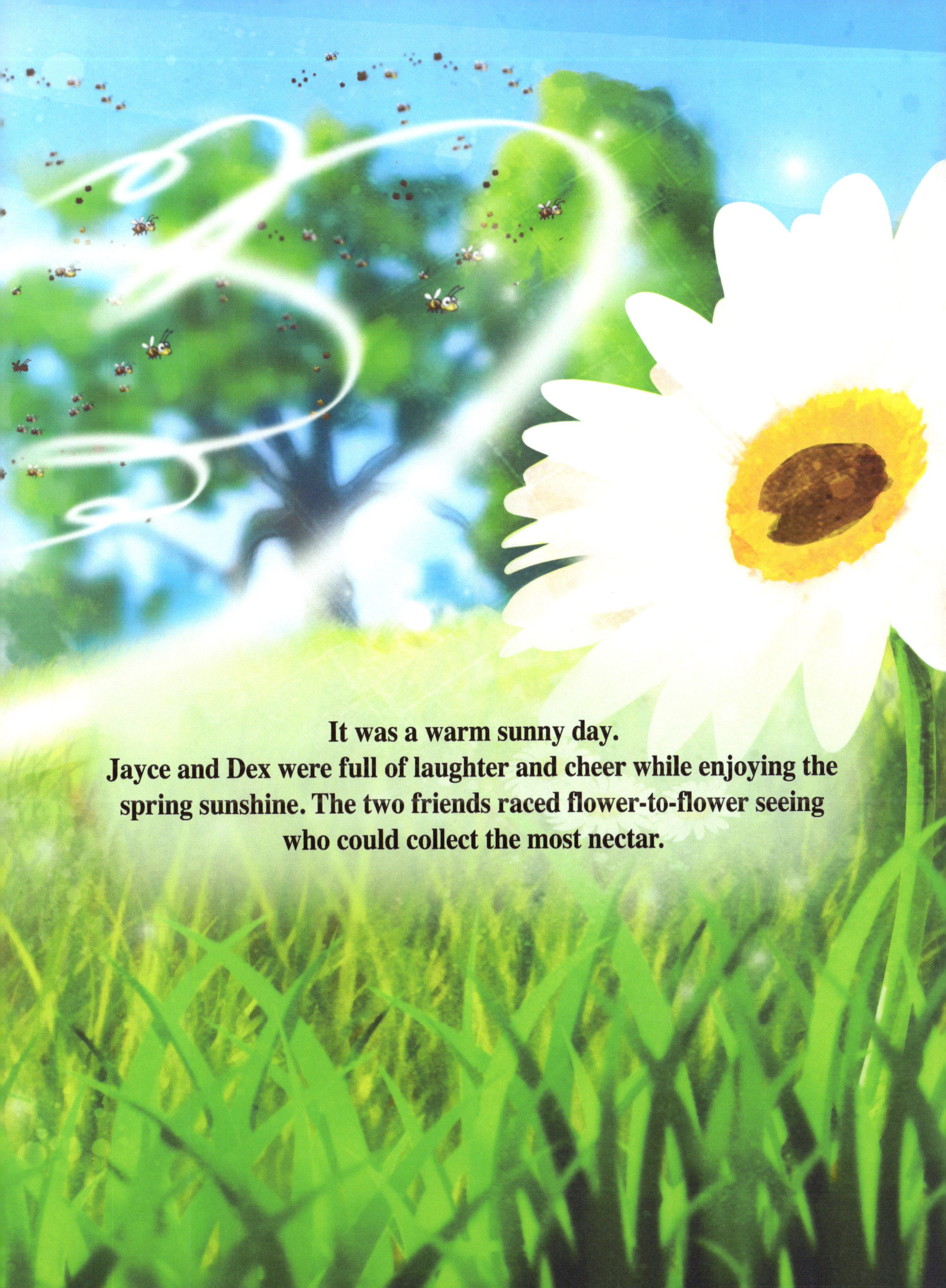

It was a warm sunny day.
Jayce and Dex were full of laughter and cheer while enjoying the spring sunshine. The two friends raced flower-to-flower seeing who could collect the most nectar.

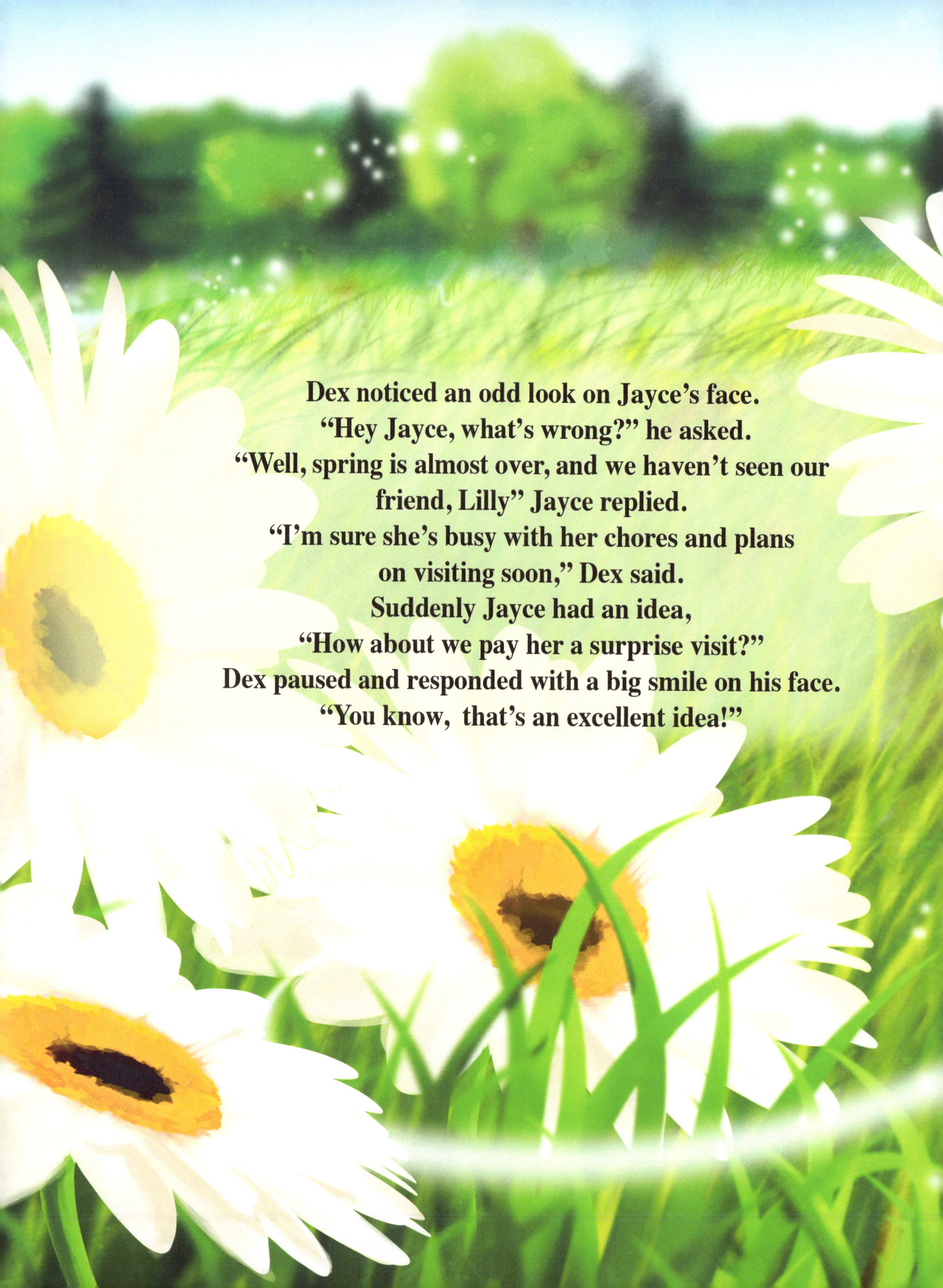

Dex noticed an odd look on Jayce's face.
"Hey Jayce, what's wrong?" he asked.
"Well, spring is almost over, and we haven't seen our friend, Lilly" Jayce replied.
"I'm sure she's busy with her chores and plans on visiting soon," Dex said.
Suddenly Jayce had an idea,
"How about we pay her a surprise visit?"
Dex paused and responded with a big smile on his face.
"You know, that's an excellent idea!"

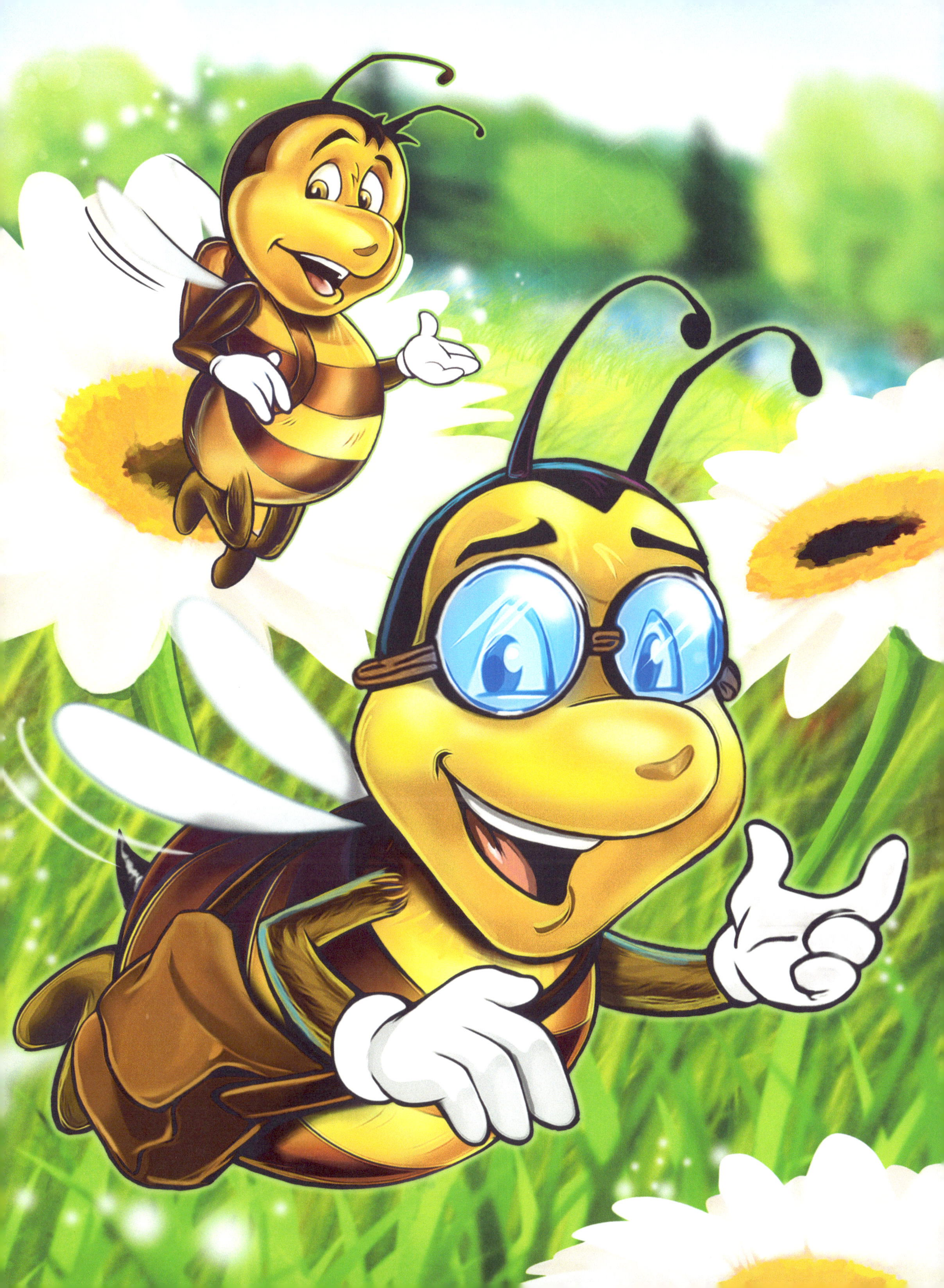

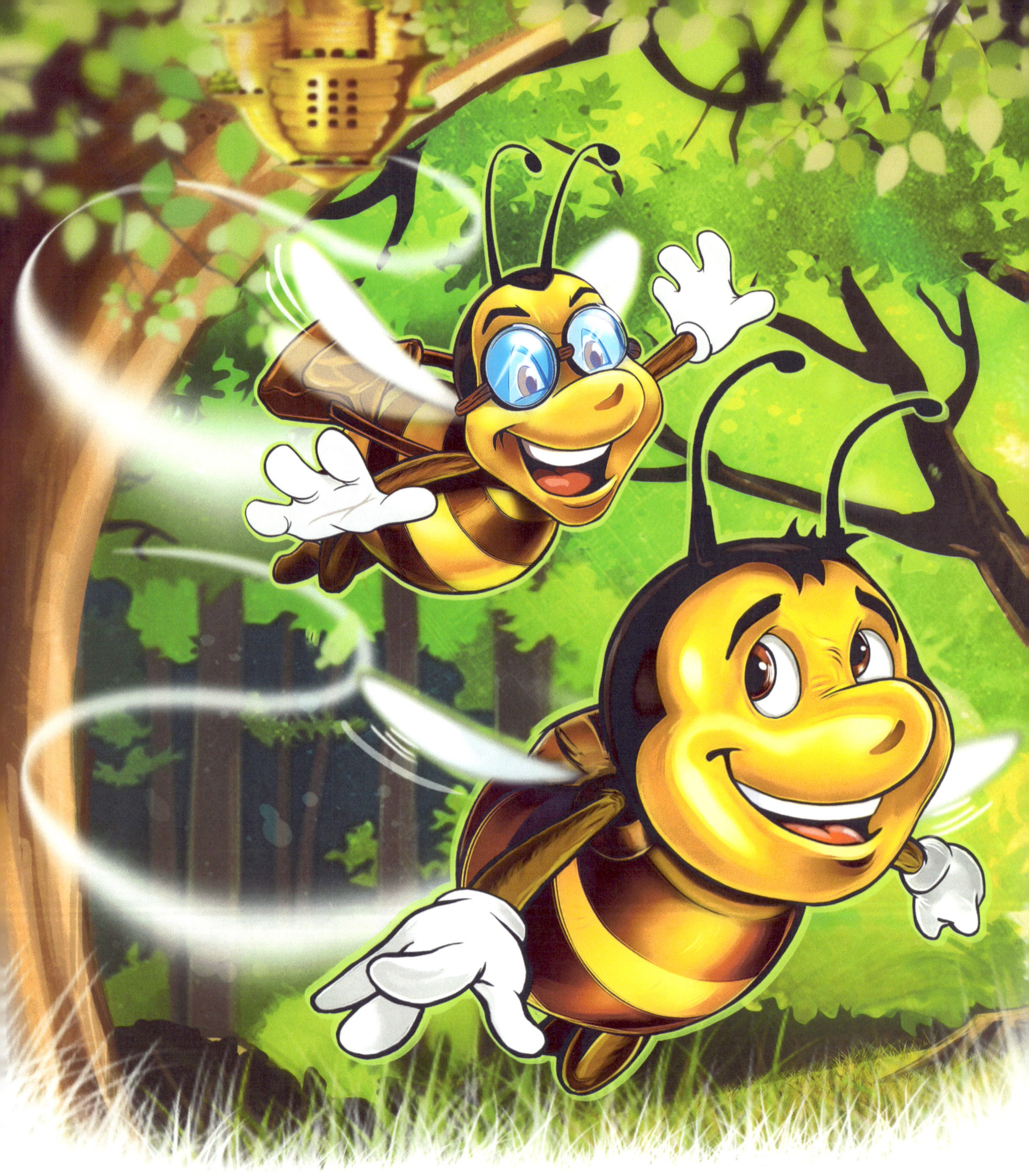

The next day, the two honey bees flew through the forest, eager to visit their ladybug friend. Lilly lives in a hidden place deep within the forest called, Polka-Dot Village.

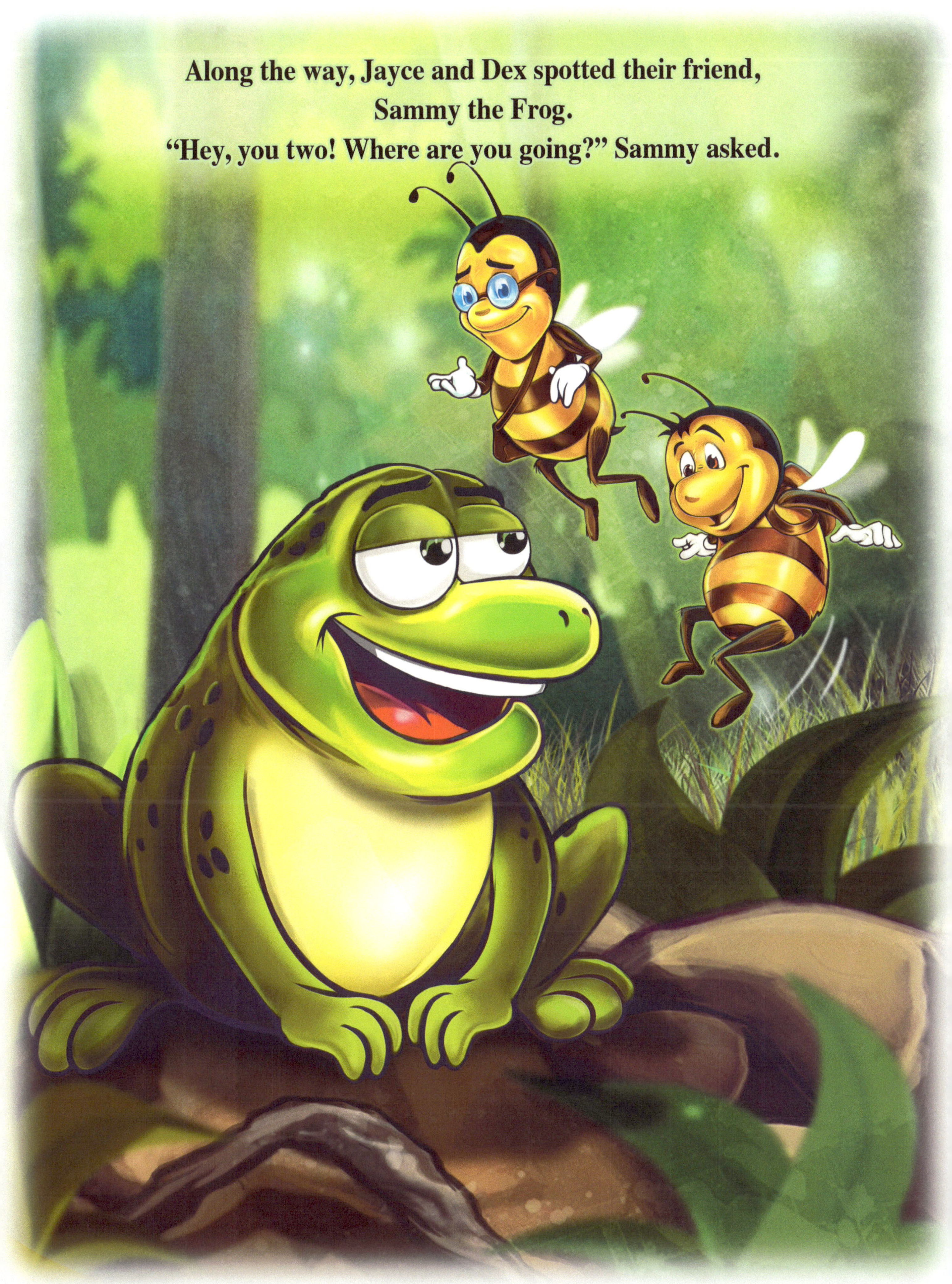

Along the way, Jayce and Dex spotted their friend,
Sammy the Frog.
"Hey, you two! Where are you going?" Sammy asked.

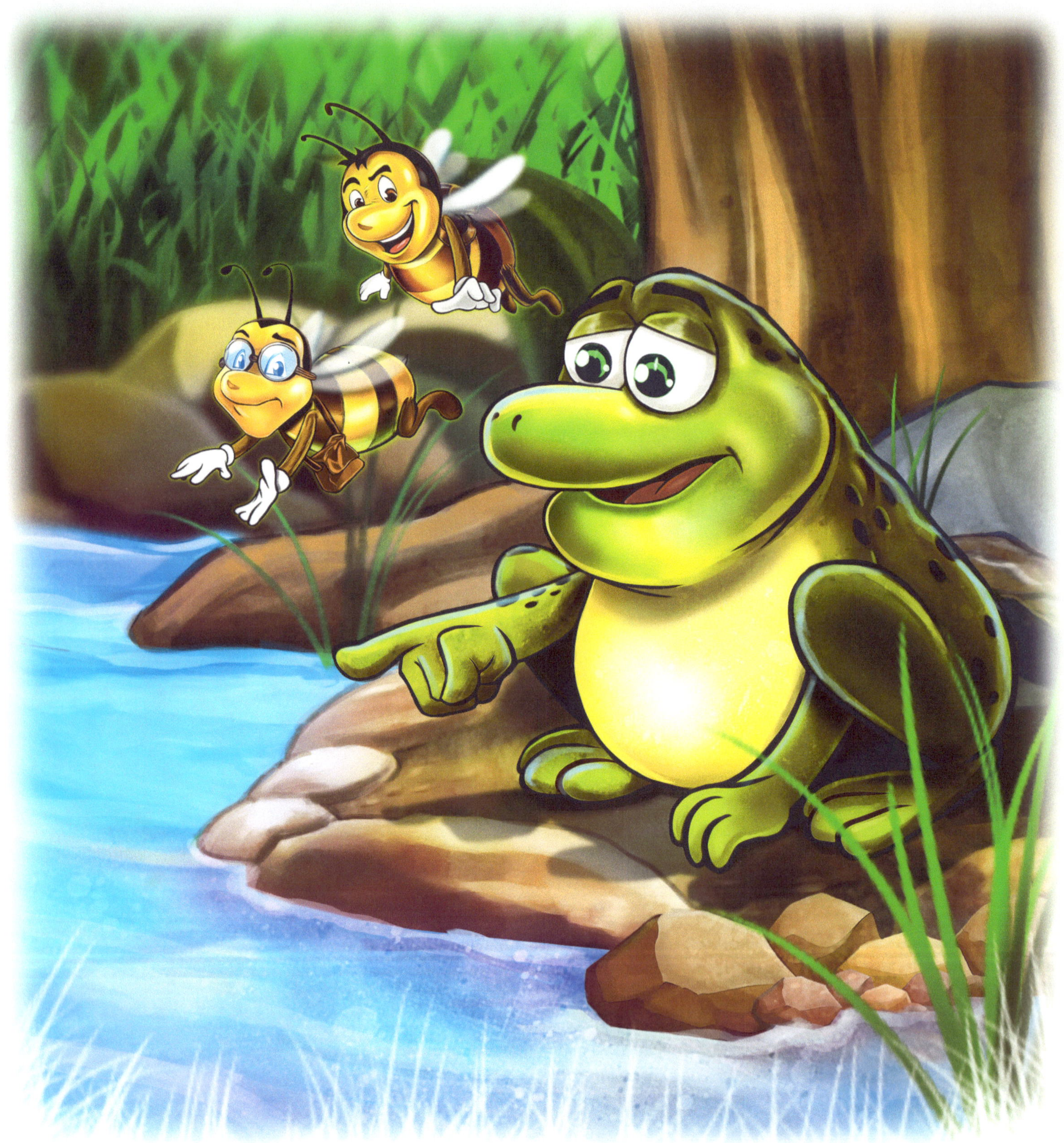

"We're on our way to visit a friend," Jayce replied.
Sammy blushed and said.
"I'm having a hard time getting to the other side of this pond.
Could you guys help me out?"
"Always happy to help a friend in need!" Jayce answered.

Dex swiftly flew over to a large petal on the ground.
"If we place this in the center of the pond, Sammy can jump to it and then to the other side," Dex explained.
"That's a great idea!" Jayce said.
The two friends carried the petal to the middle of the pond.

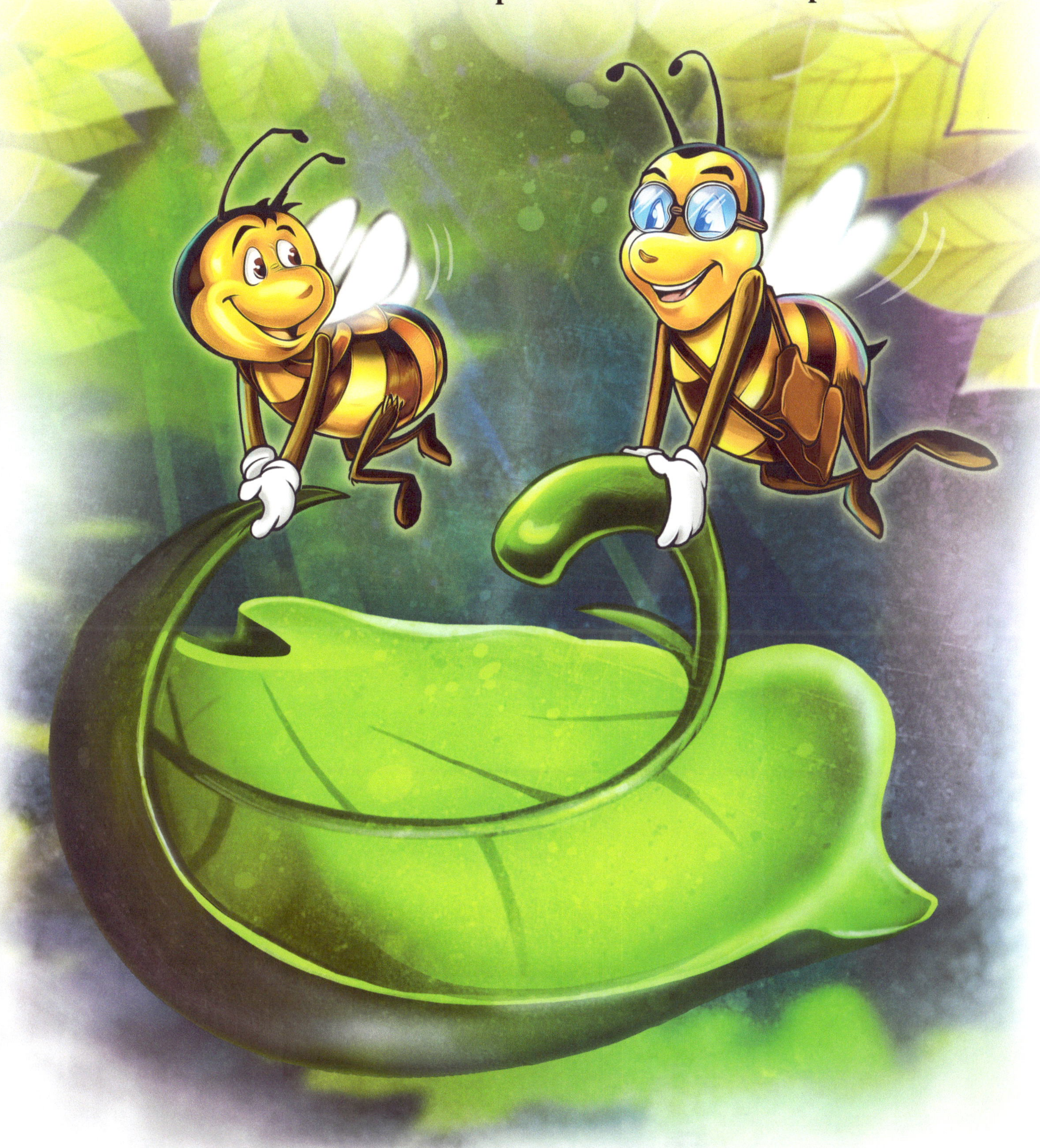

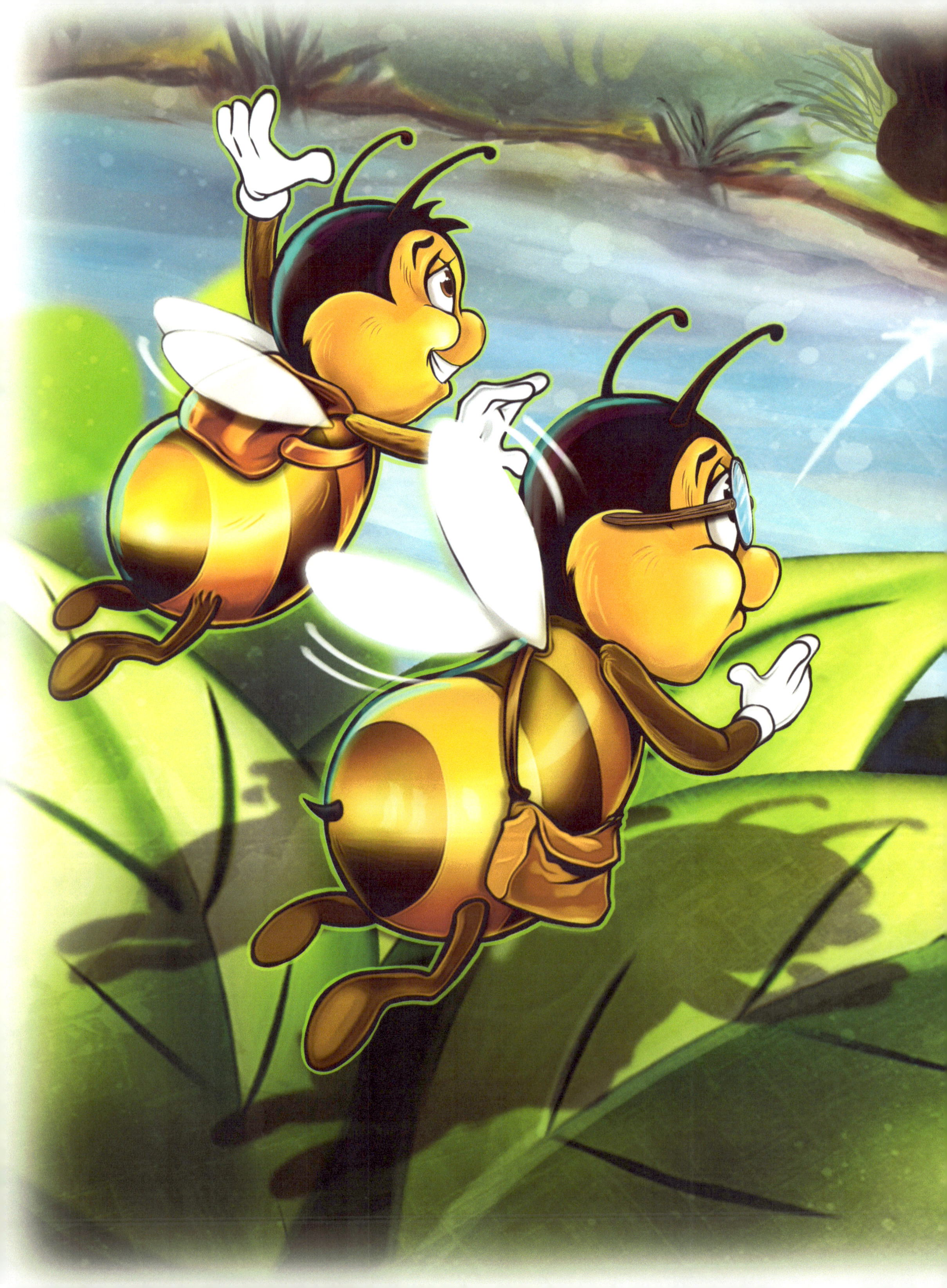

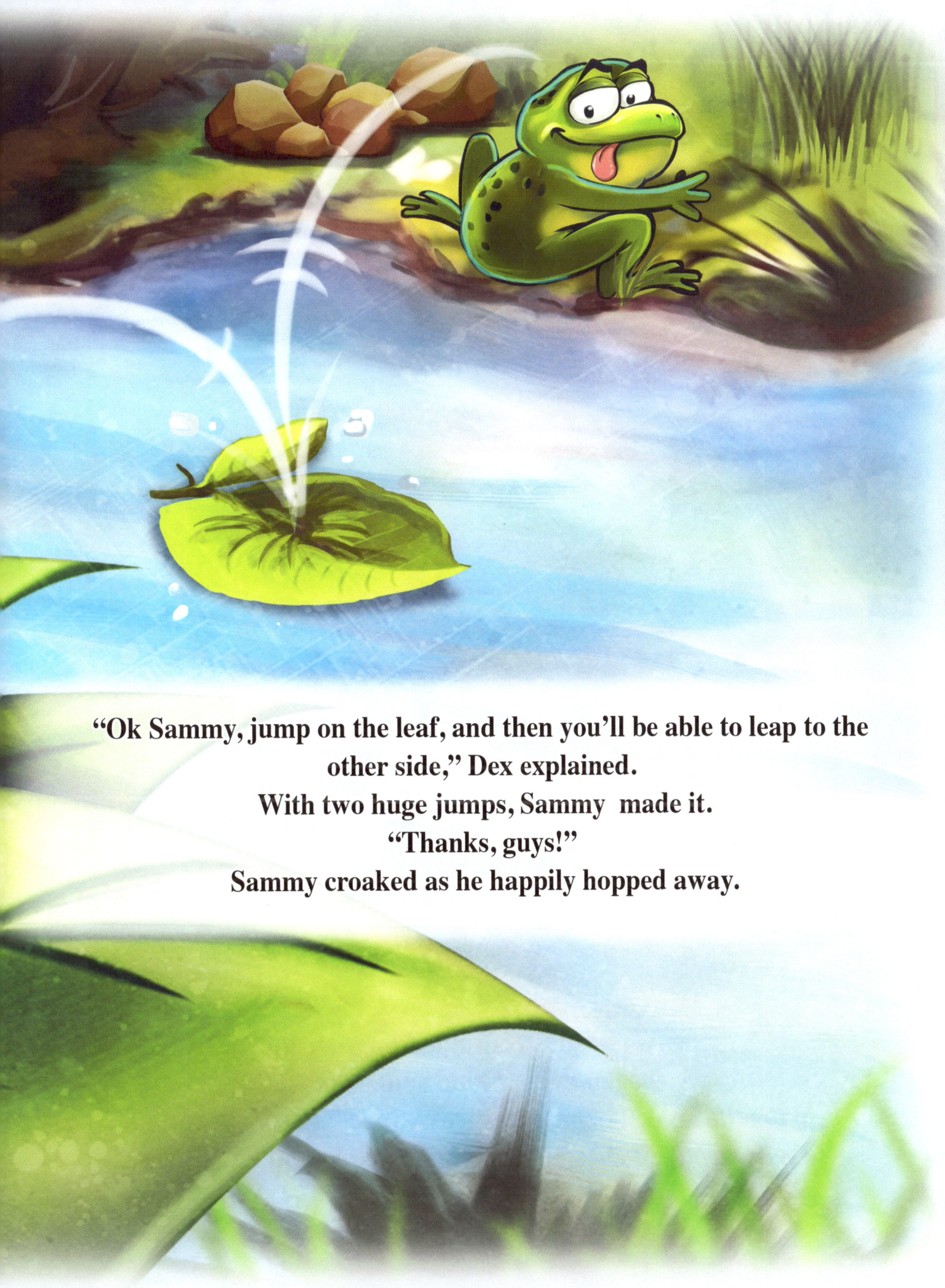

"Ok Sammy, jump on the leaf, and then you'll be able to leap to the other side," Dex explained.

With two huge jumps, Sammy made it.

"Thanks, guys!"

Sammy croaked as he happily hopped away.

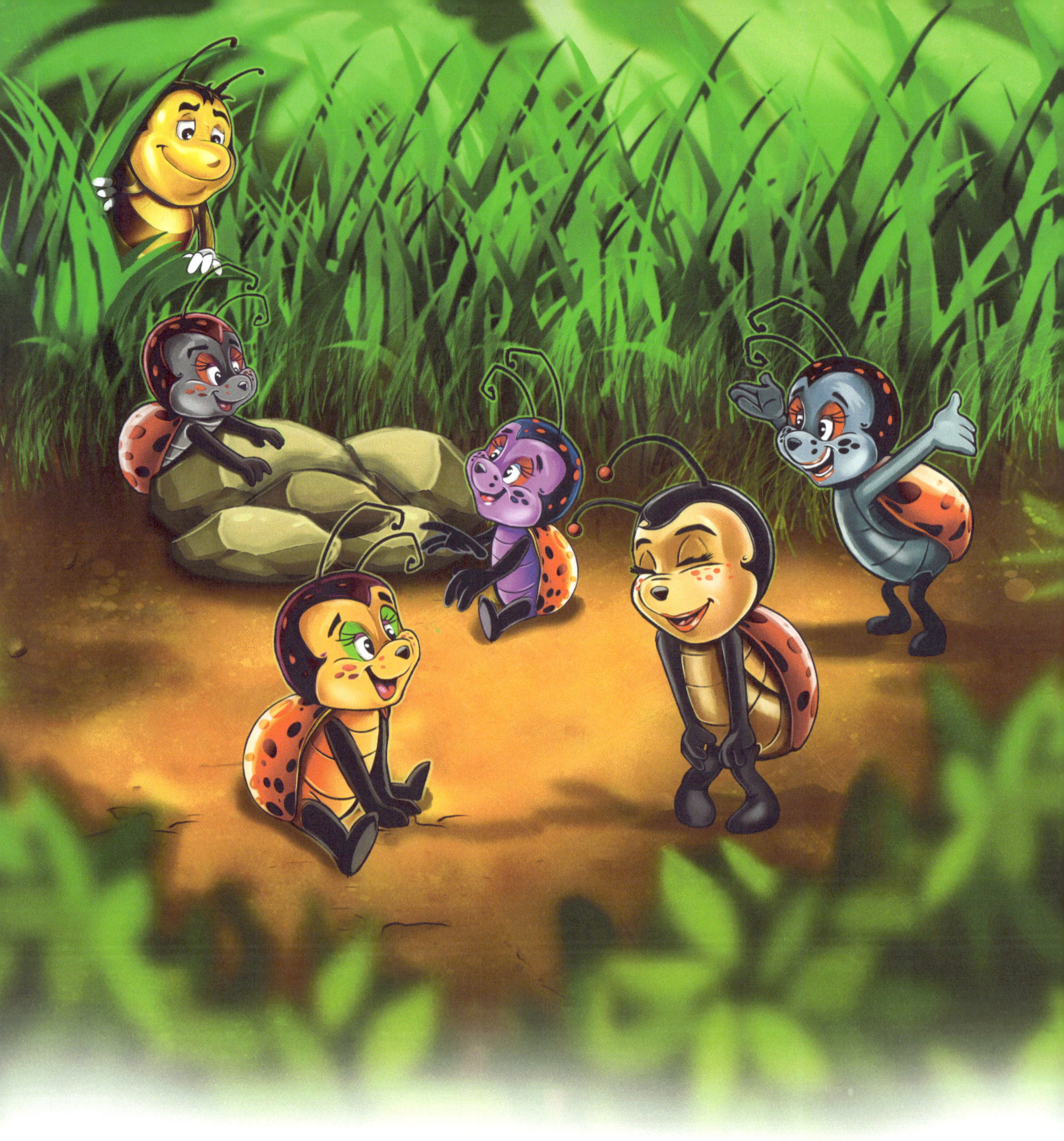

As the two friends continued on their journey, Jayce began to hear loud sounds of chatter. When he landed behind the grass, Jayce was surprised to see a group of cheerful Ladybugs joking and laughing.

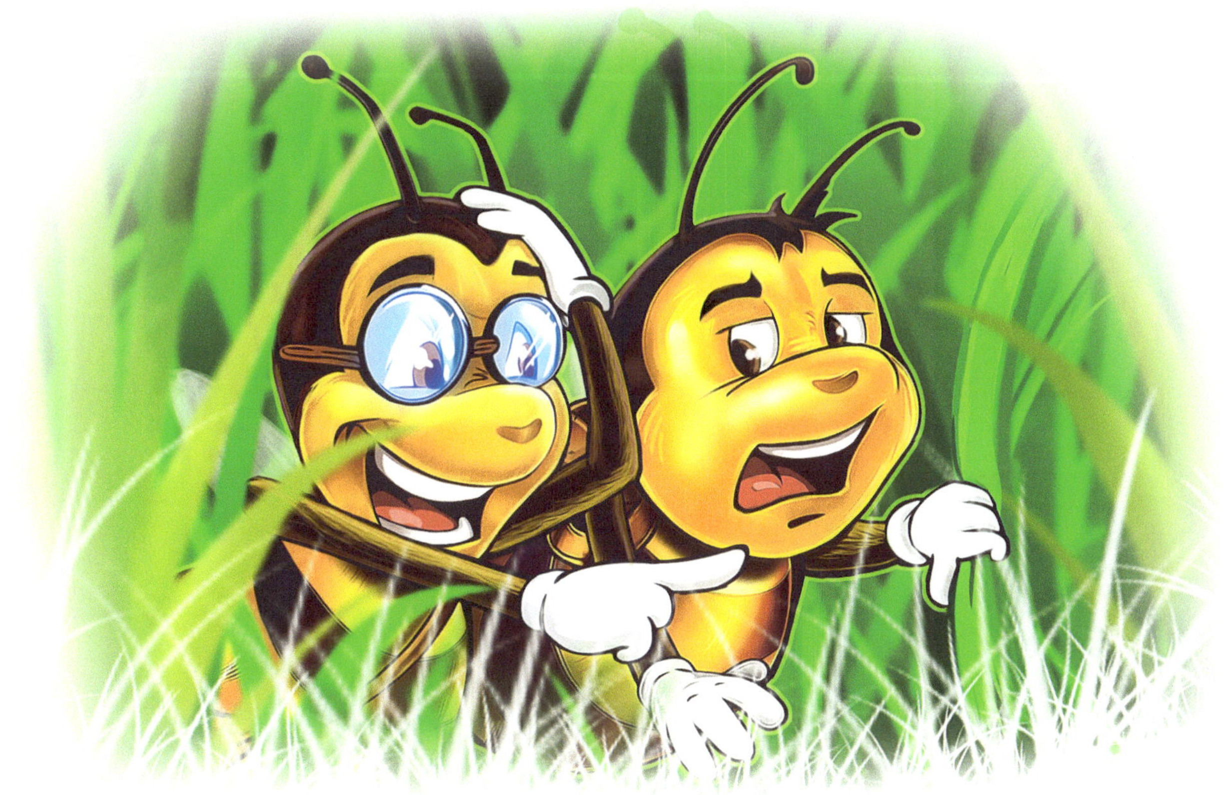

“Look, there’s Lilly over there,” Dex said with excitement.
Jayce leaped from behind the grass and shouted,

“Surprise!”

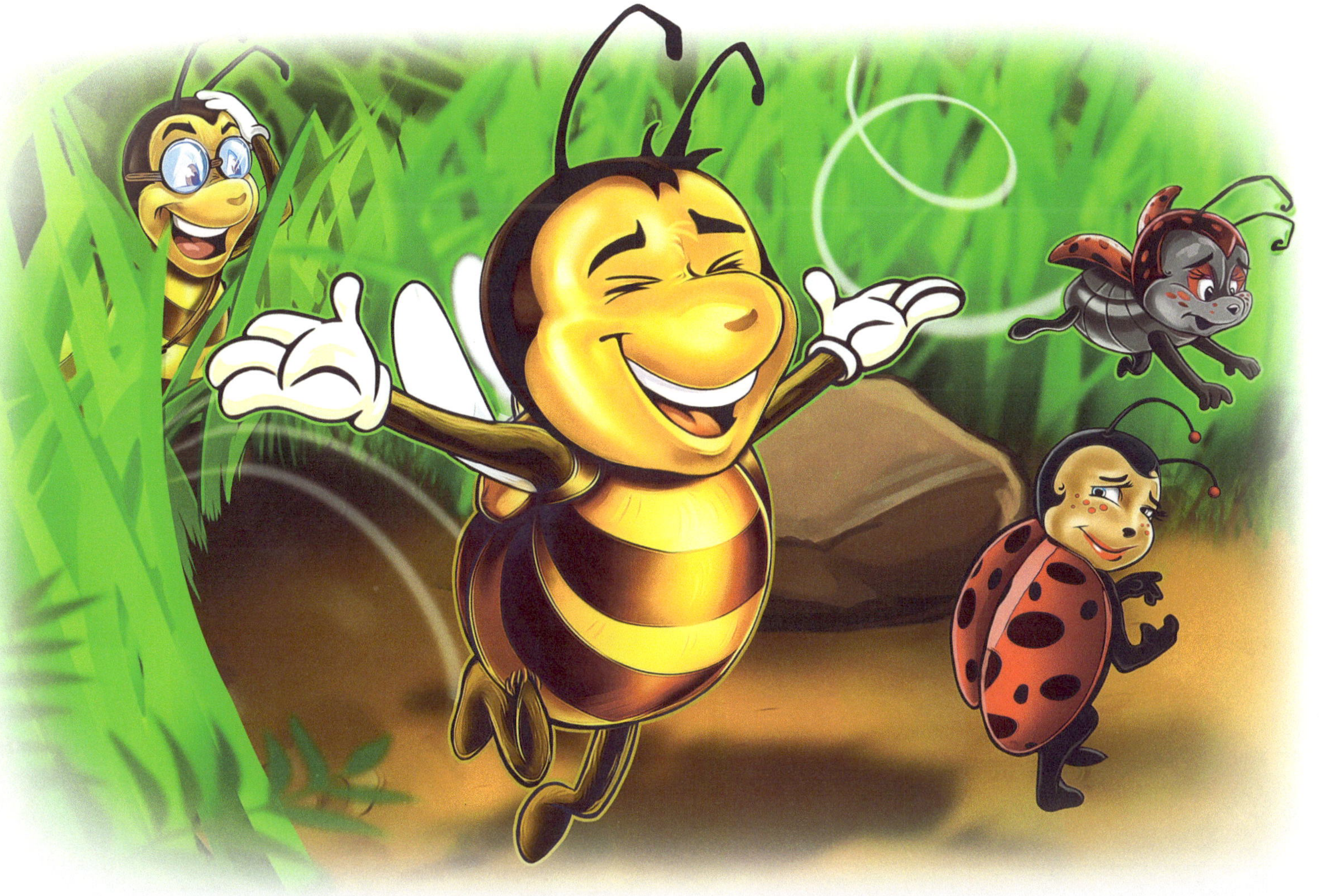

All the ladybugs scampered away in fear except for Lilly.
What are you guys doing here?" Lilly asked.
"We were worried! We haven't seen you in a while," Jayce answered.
"Why did your friends run away as if they saw a ghost?"
Dex questioned.

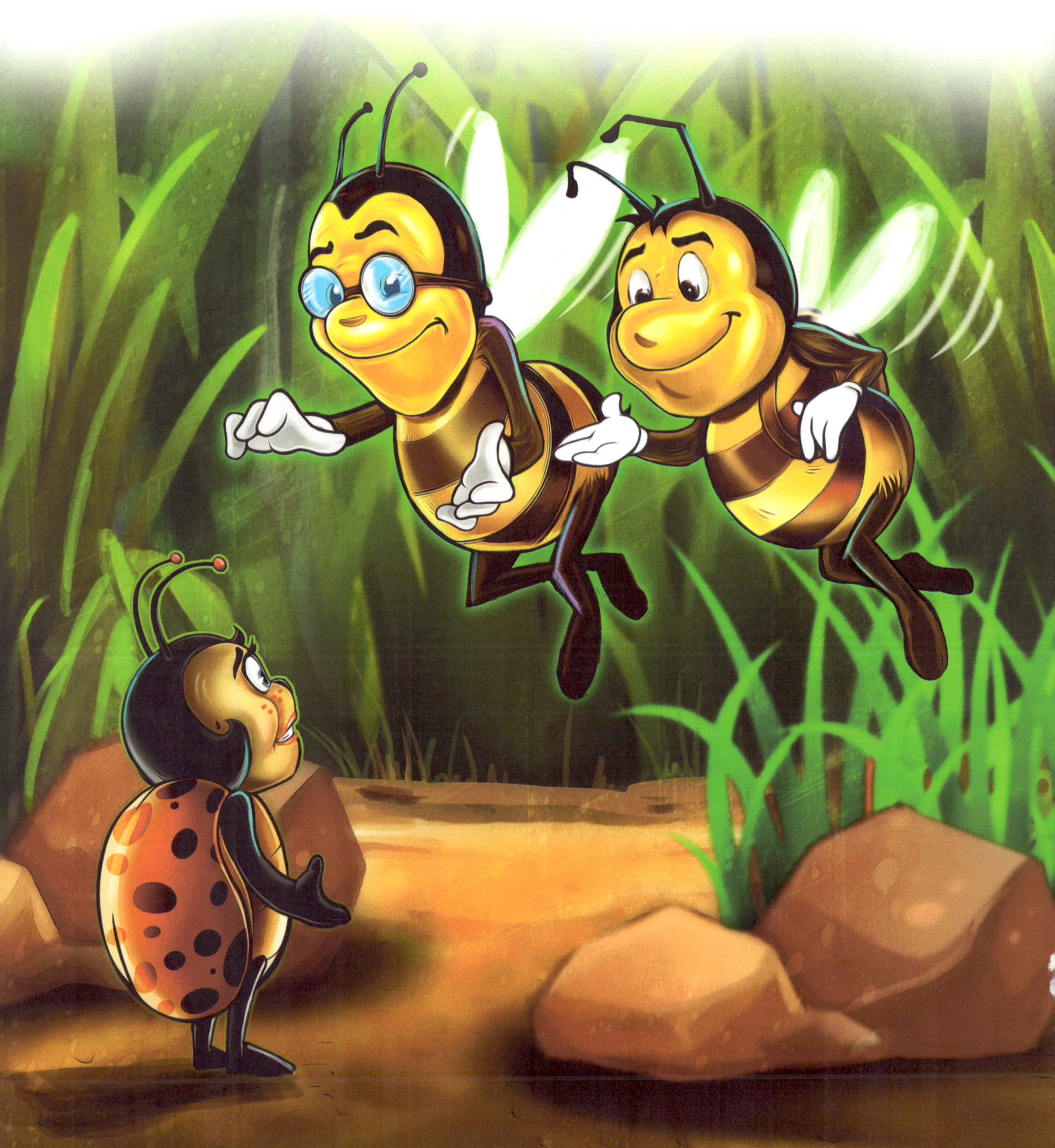

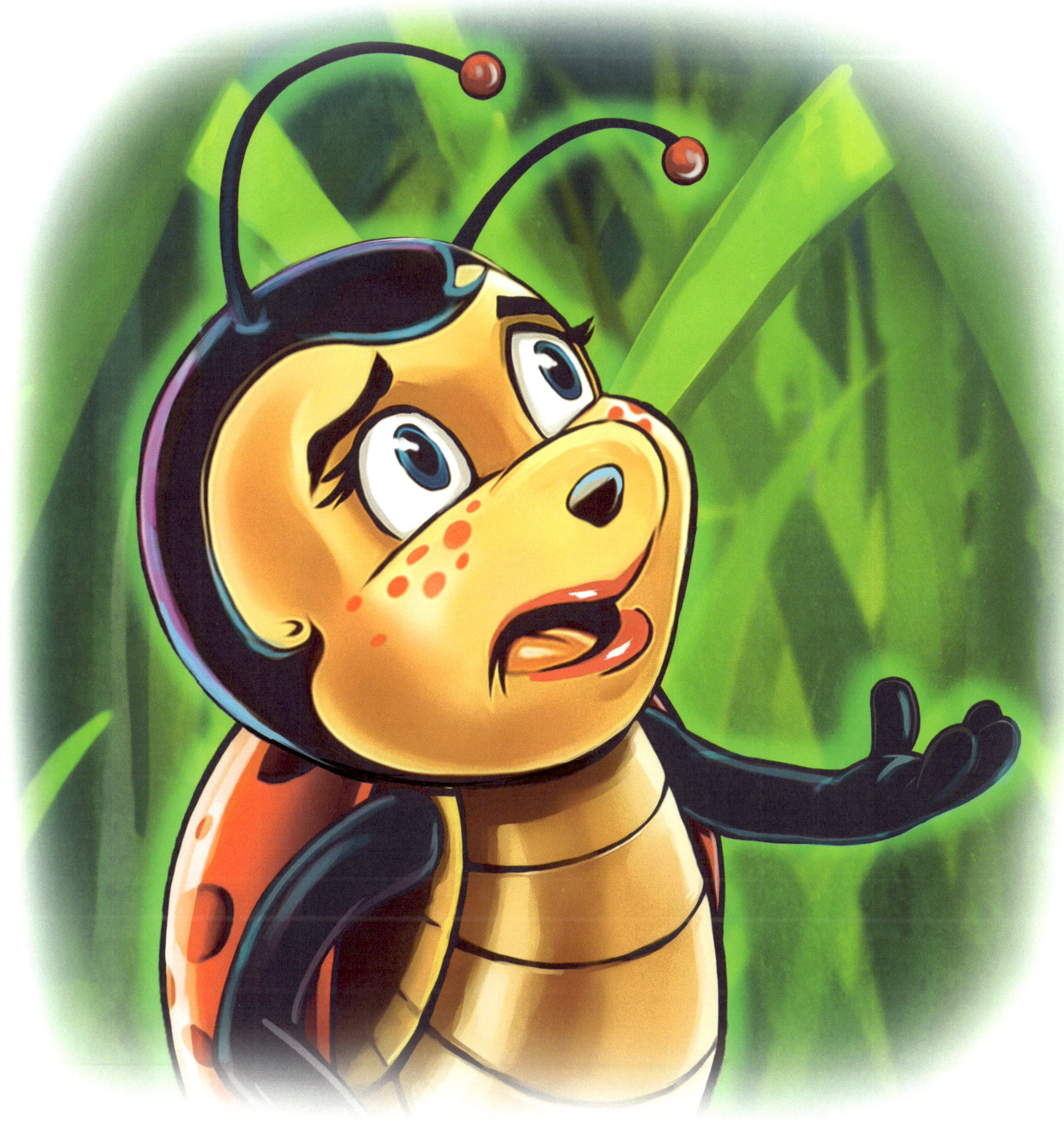

**Lilly began to explain.
"Ladybugs are not allowed to interact with bees."
Jayce and Dex stared in disbelief. "Is that why you haven't
returned to Beetopia?" Jayce asked.
"Yes," she whispered.
"The elders have forbidden me to visit."**

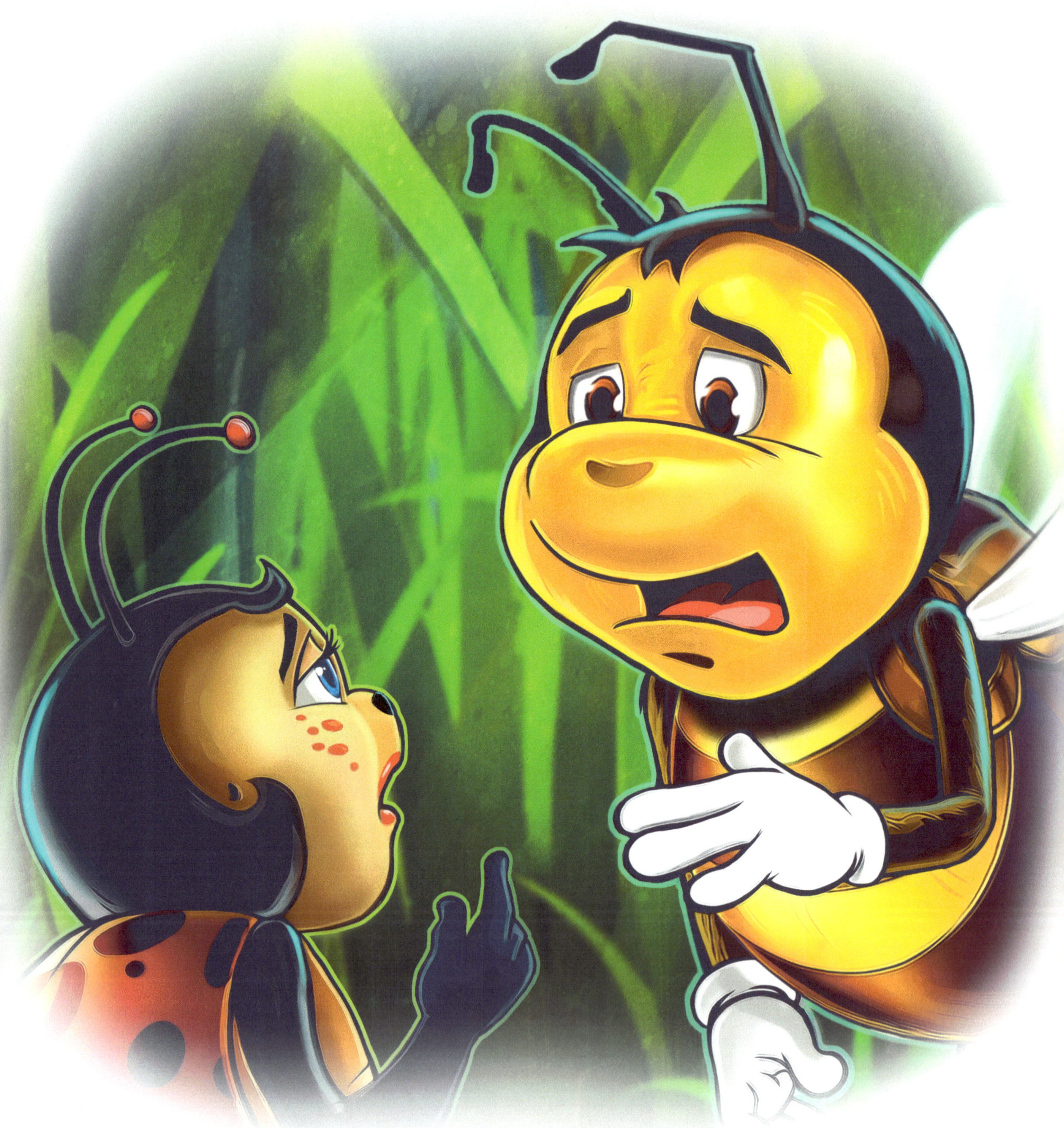

This news made Jayce and Dex very sad.
"B-but you're our friend Lilly, and all the bees of Beetopia adore you."
"Is there something we can do to change their minds?" Jayce cried.

Before Lilly could respond, the ladybugs returned with, Lady Loren, and Lady Lyla, the leaders of the Polka-Dot Village.

"Lilly are you alright? Have they harmed you?" shouted Lady Lyla.

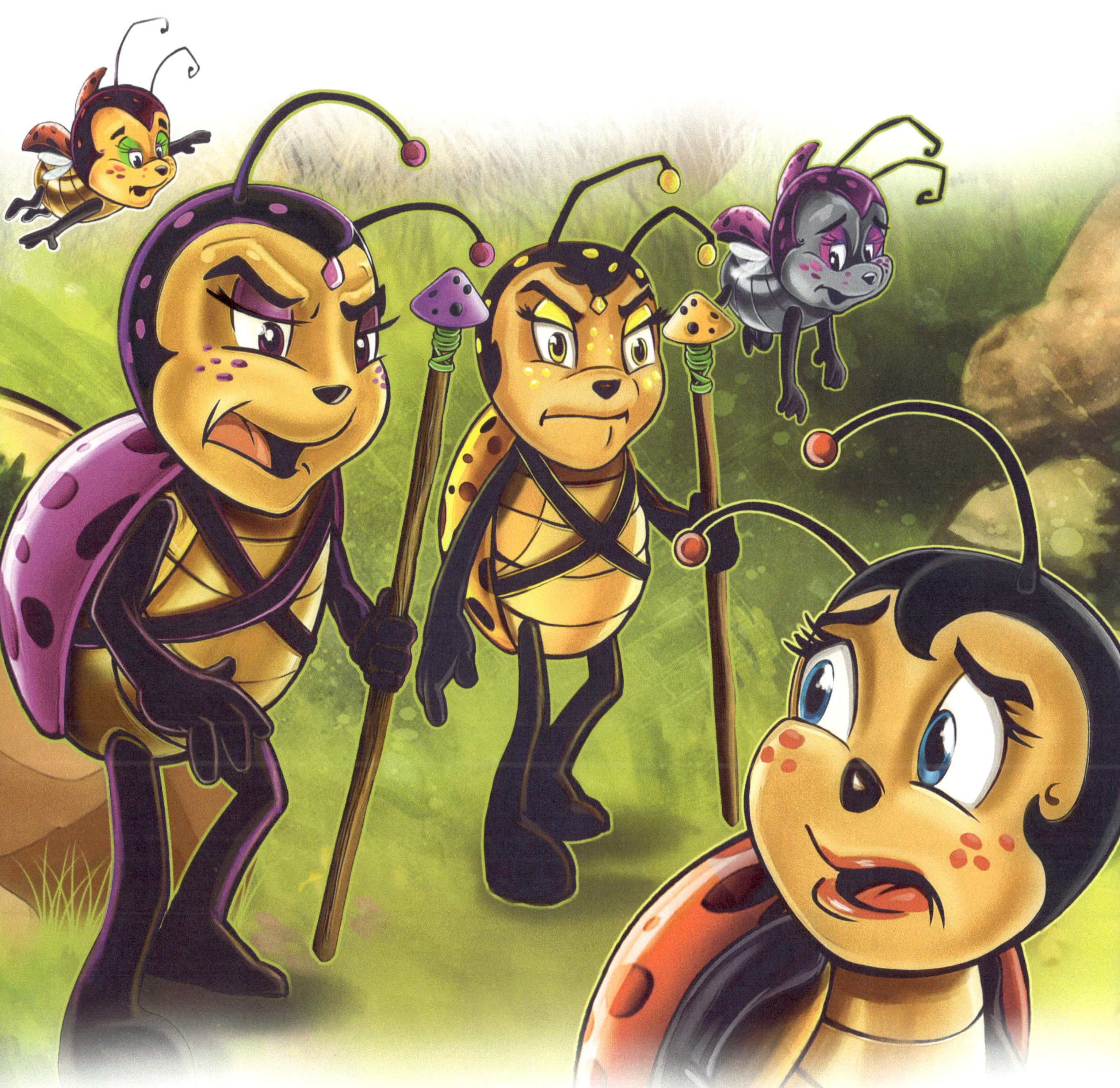

"No, I'm fine!" Lilly replied.

"Who are you, and why are you here?" Lady Loren demanded.

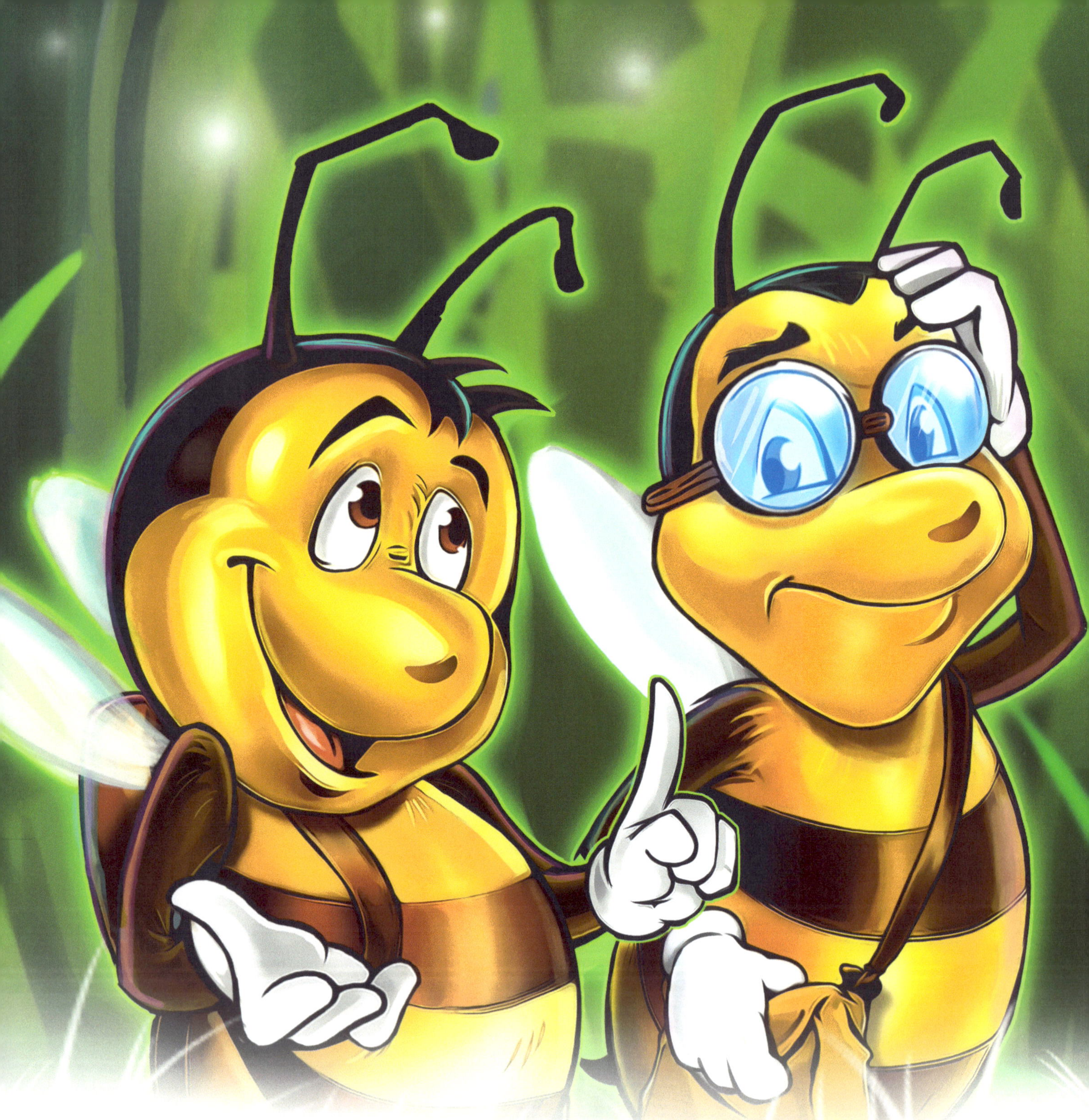

"I'm Jayce, and this is my friend Dex," Jayce answered with a smile. He nudged Dex to say something.

"Uhhh, hello," Dex murmured while avoiding eye contact.

Jayce explained that Lilly was their friend, and considered a hero in the colony of Beetopia.

The elders were very disappointed.
"Bees are dangerous, and we have no business calling them friends!"
Elder Lyla exclaimed.
"I know bees have a reputation for being mean, but it's not true!
They are kind and gentle." Lilly explained.

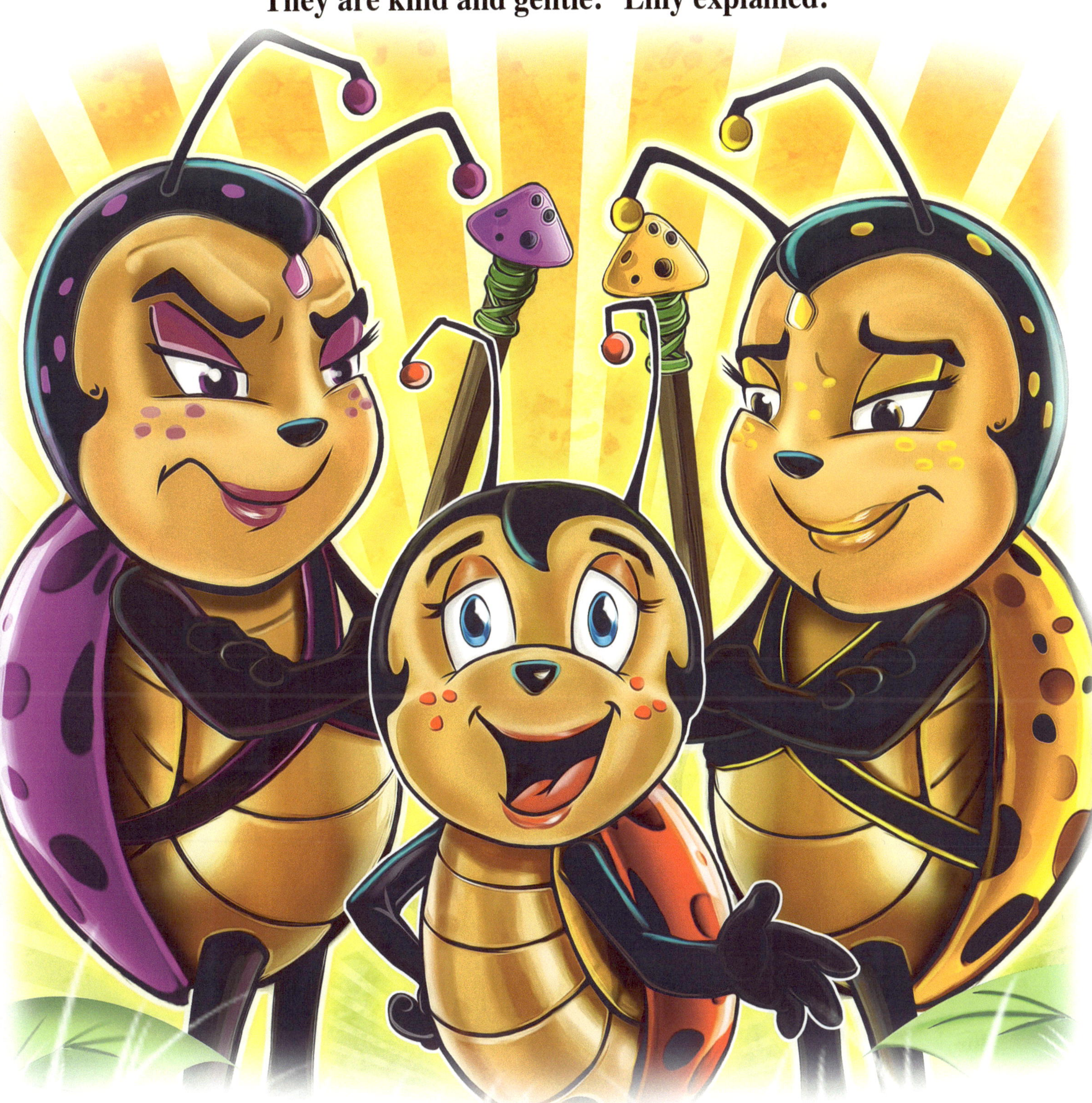

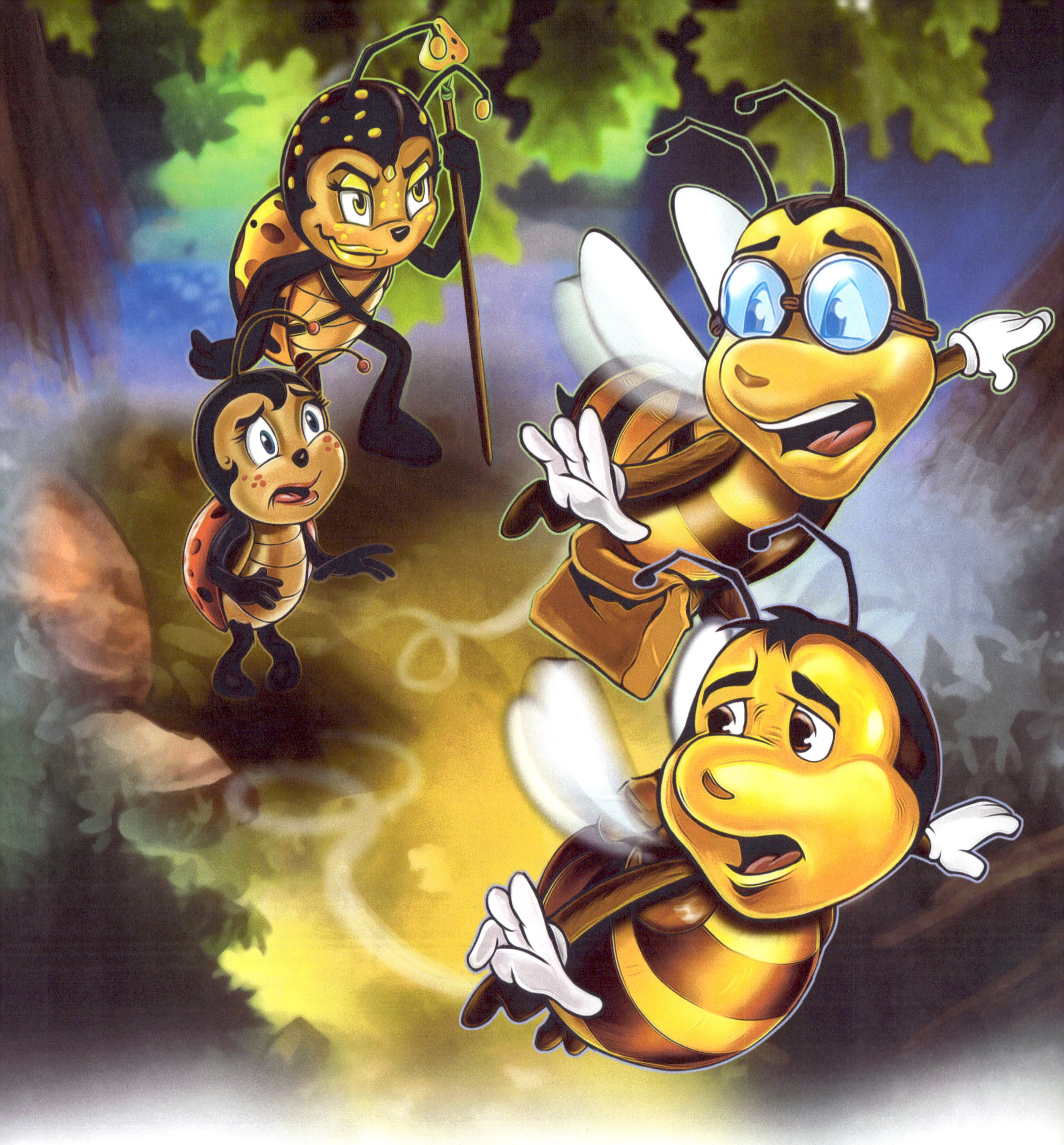

There was no convincing the elders.
"You are not welcome here and must leave now!"
Loren declared.
Jayce and Dex waved goodbye as they began to fly away.

Suddenly, a large shadow flew overhead.
Everyone stood frozen with fear. It was three large dragonflies, and they were flying right towards the ladybugs!
"Everyone get back to the village now!" Shouted Elder Loren.
The ladybugs scattered as the dragonflies began to attack.

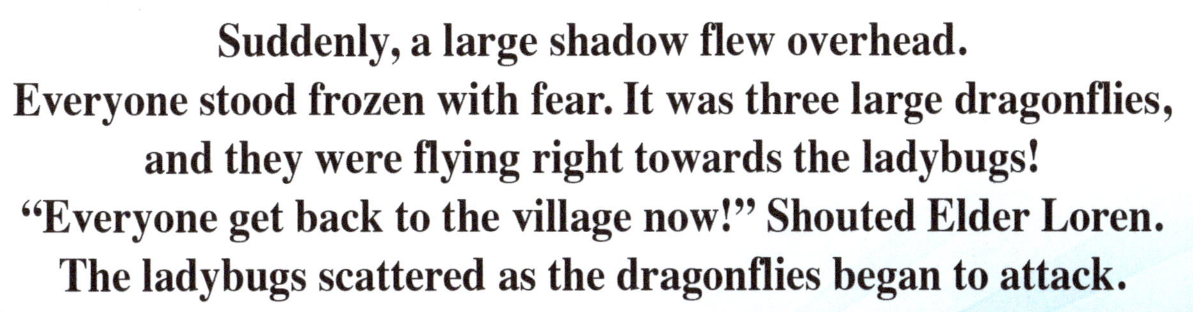

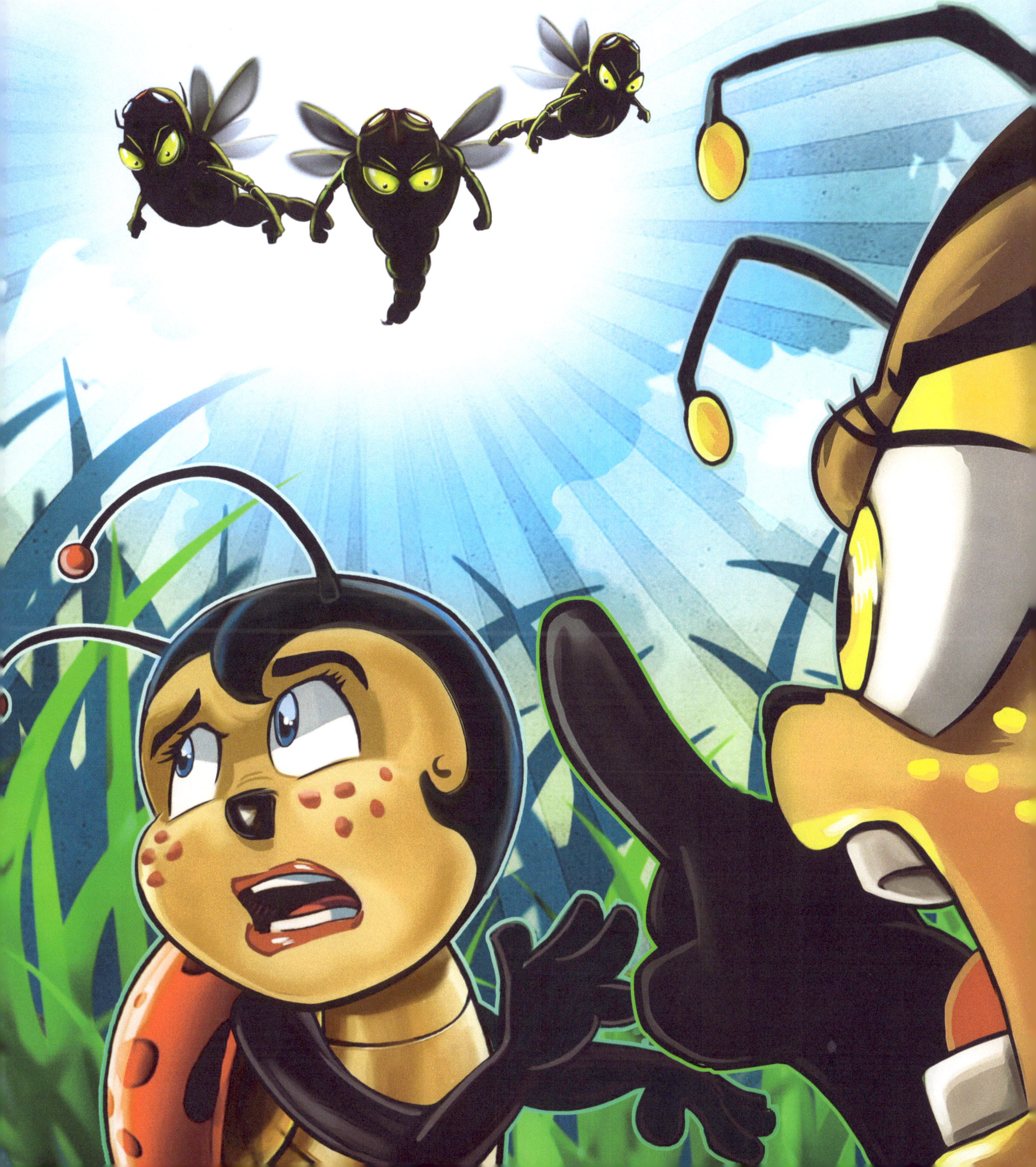

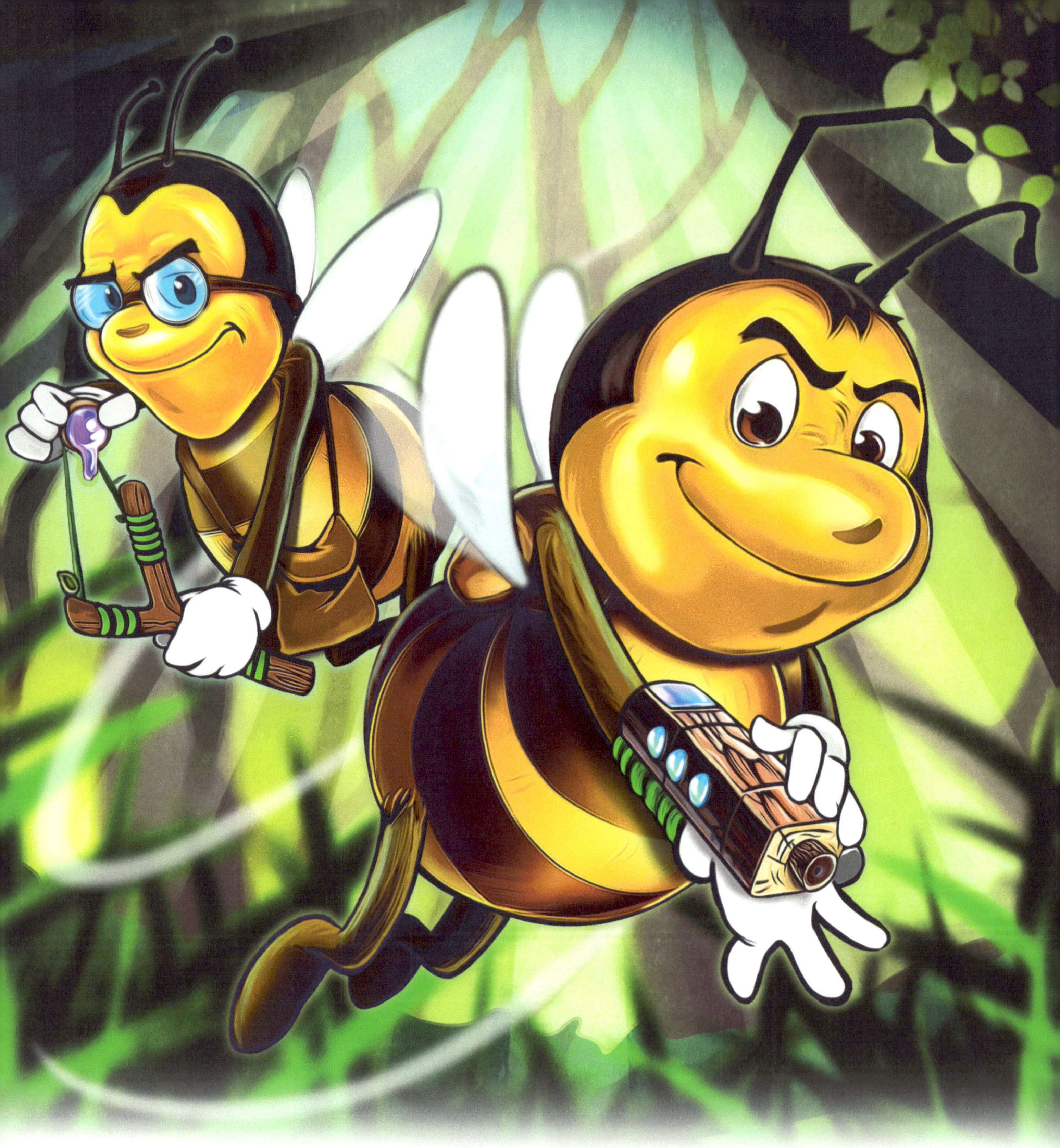

"Dex, we have to help them! I'll distract the dragonflies, while you help everyone get to safety!" Jayce exclaimed as he strapped on his magical brace. "Okay!" Dex responded.

Dex splattered one of the dragonflies with his slingshot.
"Over here!" Jayce shouted.
The remaining dragonflies began to chase after Jayce.
He was able to lead them away from the ladybugs.

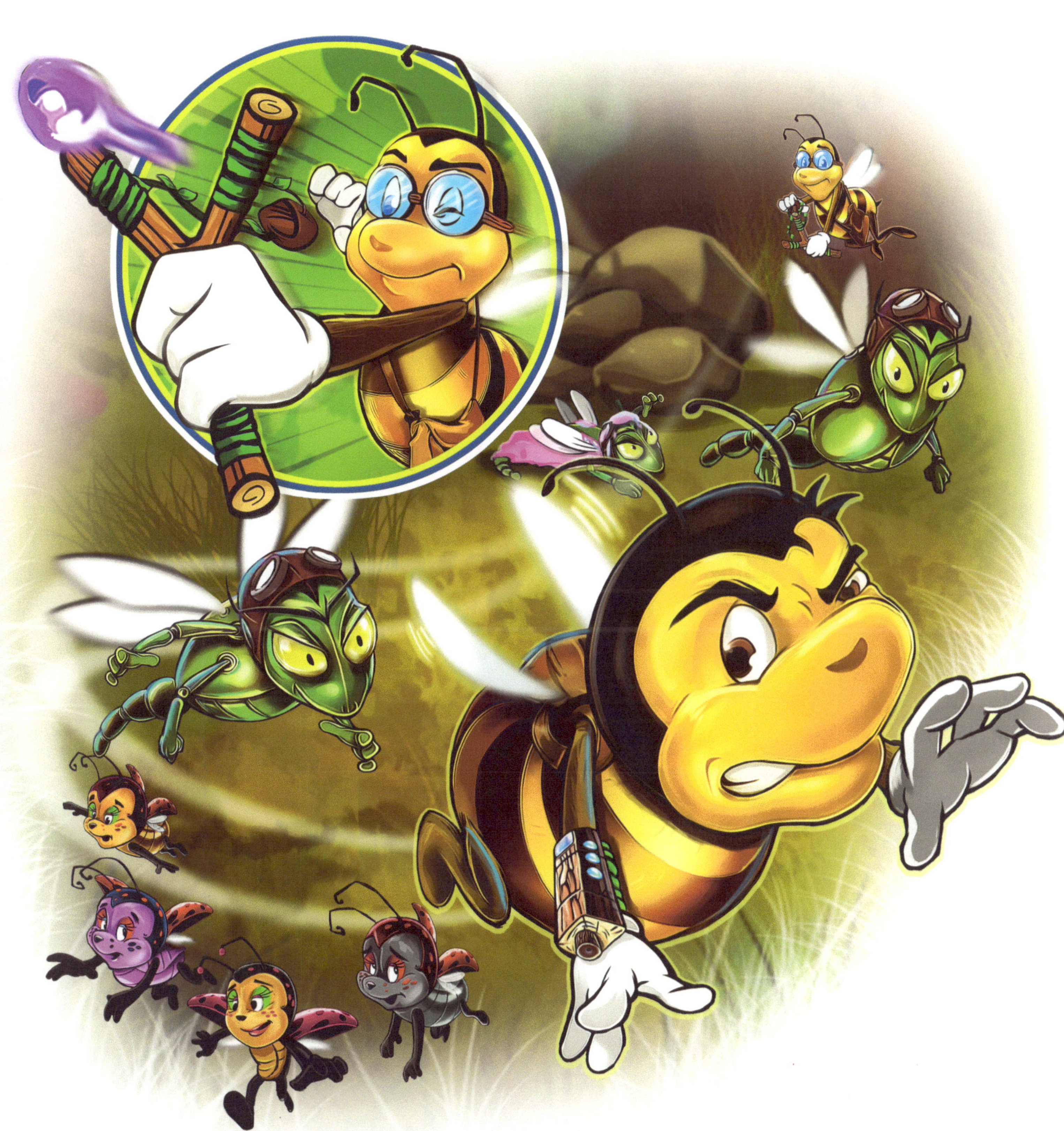

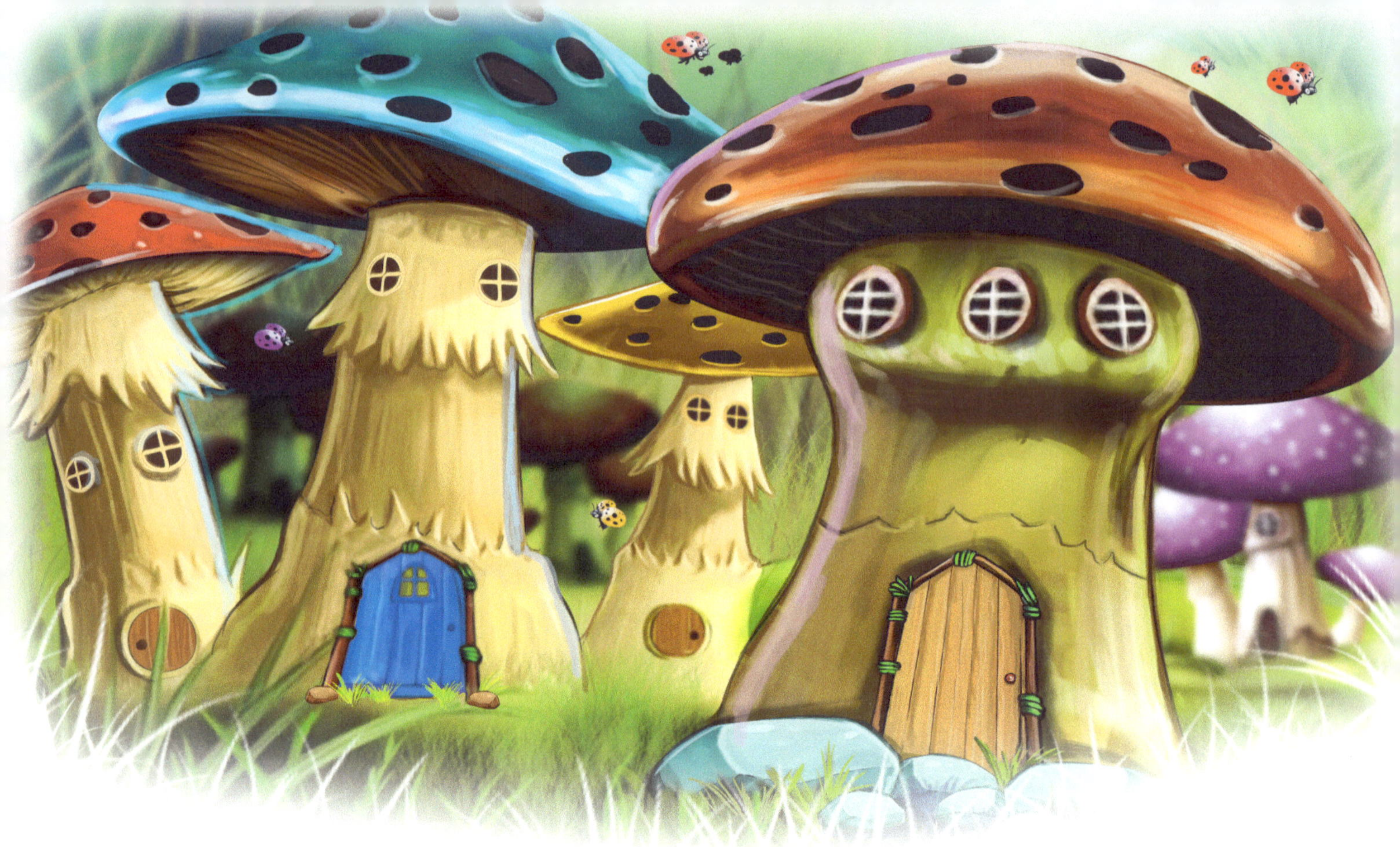

Meanwhile, Dex helped Lilly and her friends return safely to the Polka-Dot Village.
"Is everyone ok?" Dex asked.
Lilly responded, "Everyone seems fine, but where's Jayce?"
"He lured the dragonflies into the forest," Dex answered.

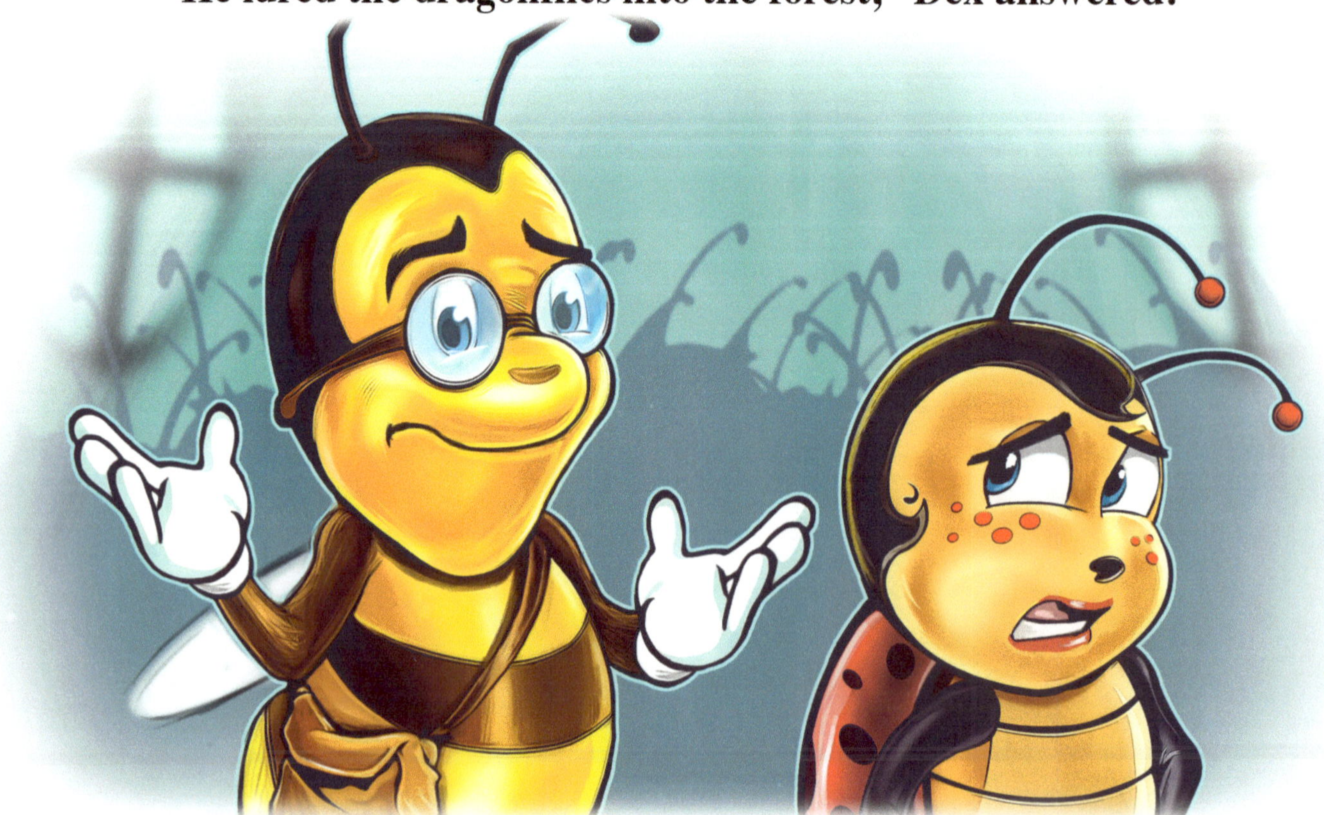

"He could be in big trouble. We have to help him!"
Lilly exclaimed.
Lady Loren nodded and said, "You have our permission."
Lilly pulled out her Wind Dasher, but before she could say another word,
Dex grabbed her hand and sped off into the forest.

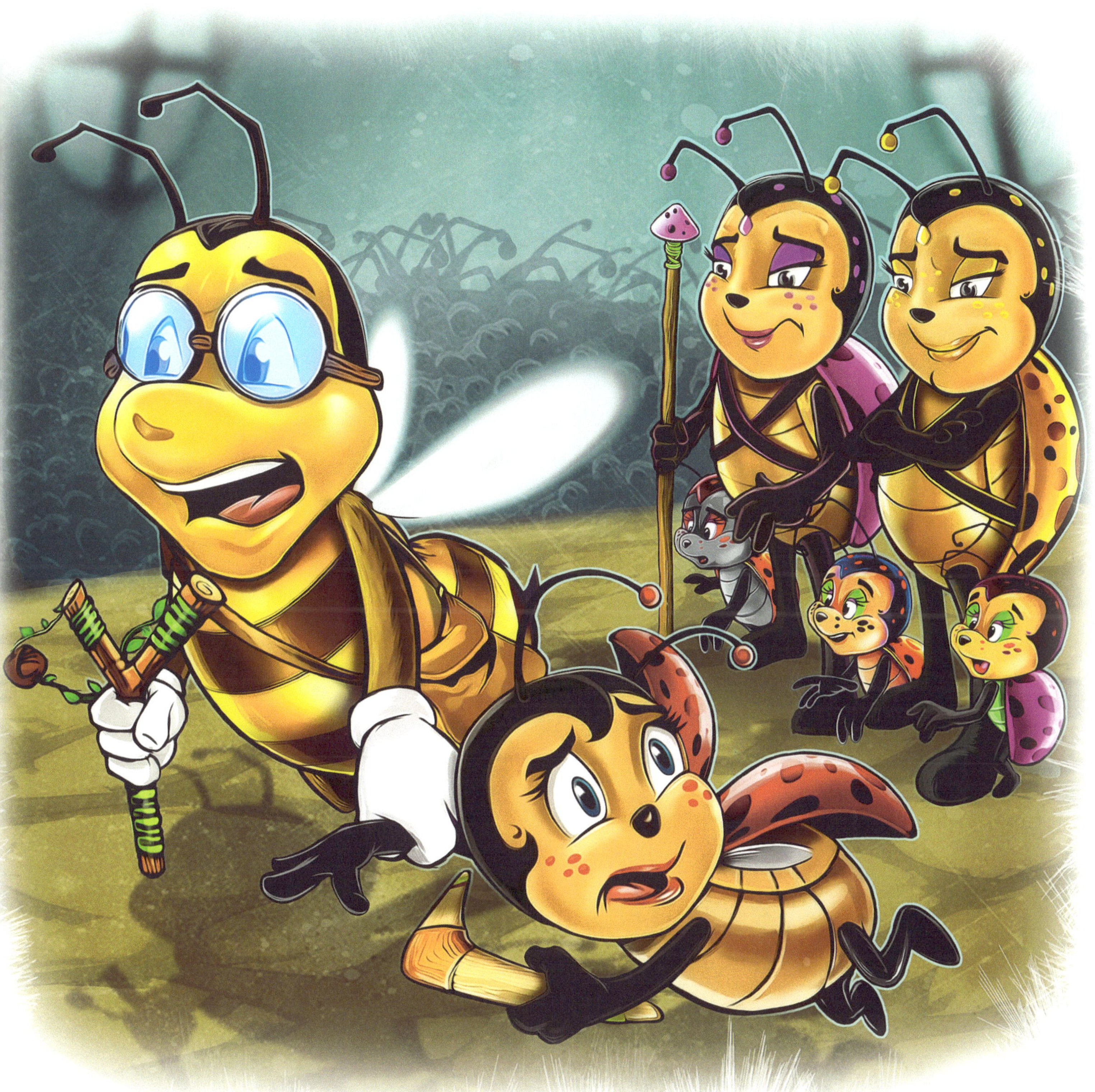

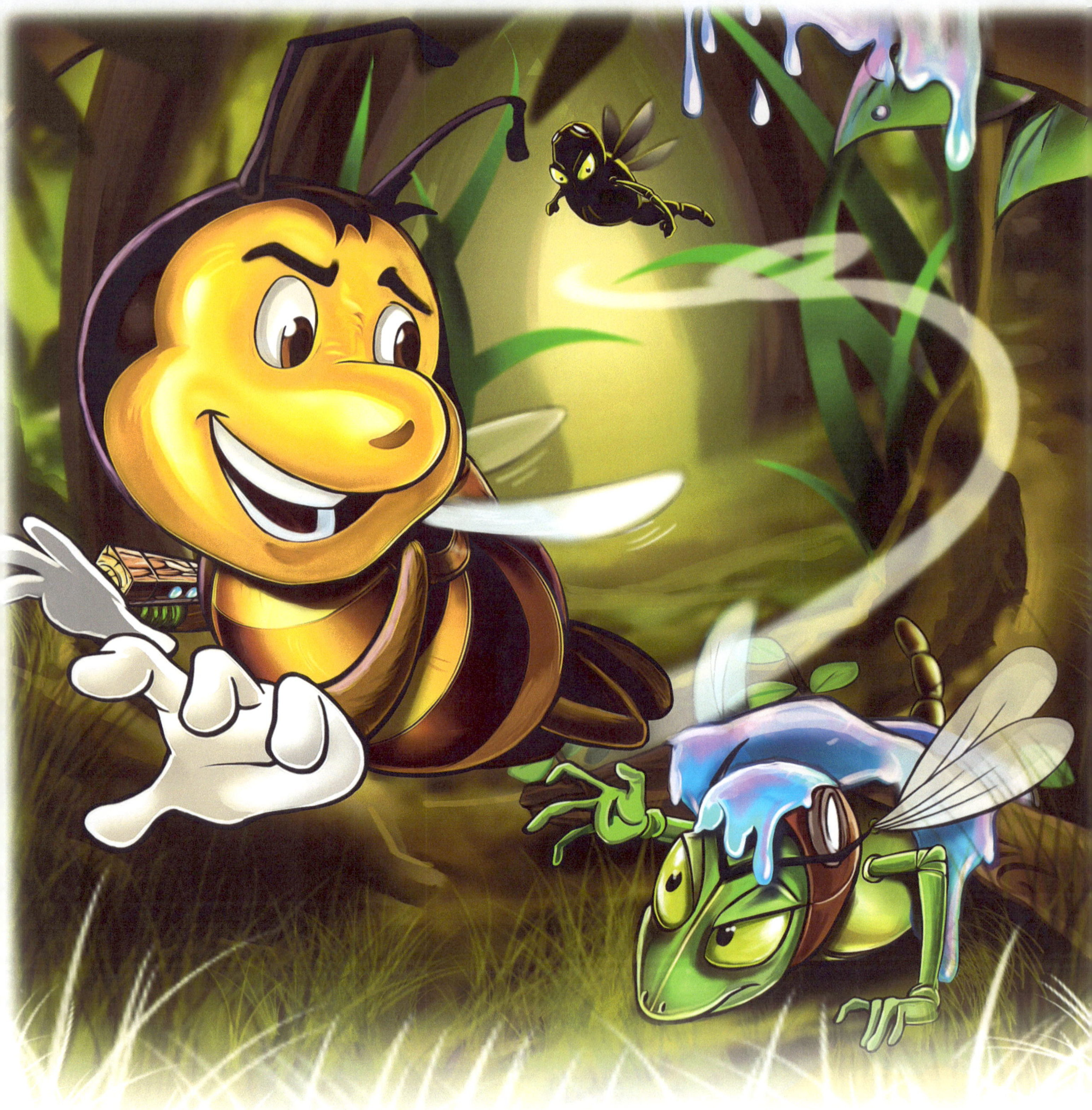

Meanwhile, Jayce zoomed through the woods with the dragonflies in hot pursuit.

He aimed his magical brace and sprayed an oncoming tree branch with treesha, causing it to fall on top of the trailing dragonfly.

“One down, one to go!” Jayce cheered.

The last dragonfly grabbed Jayce in mid-air and threw him to the ground. "When I finish with you," chuckled the dragonfly, "I'll go back and finish those tasty ladybugs!"

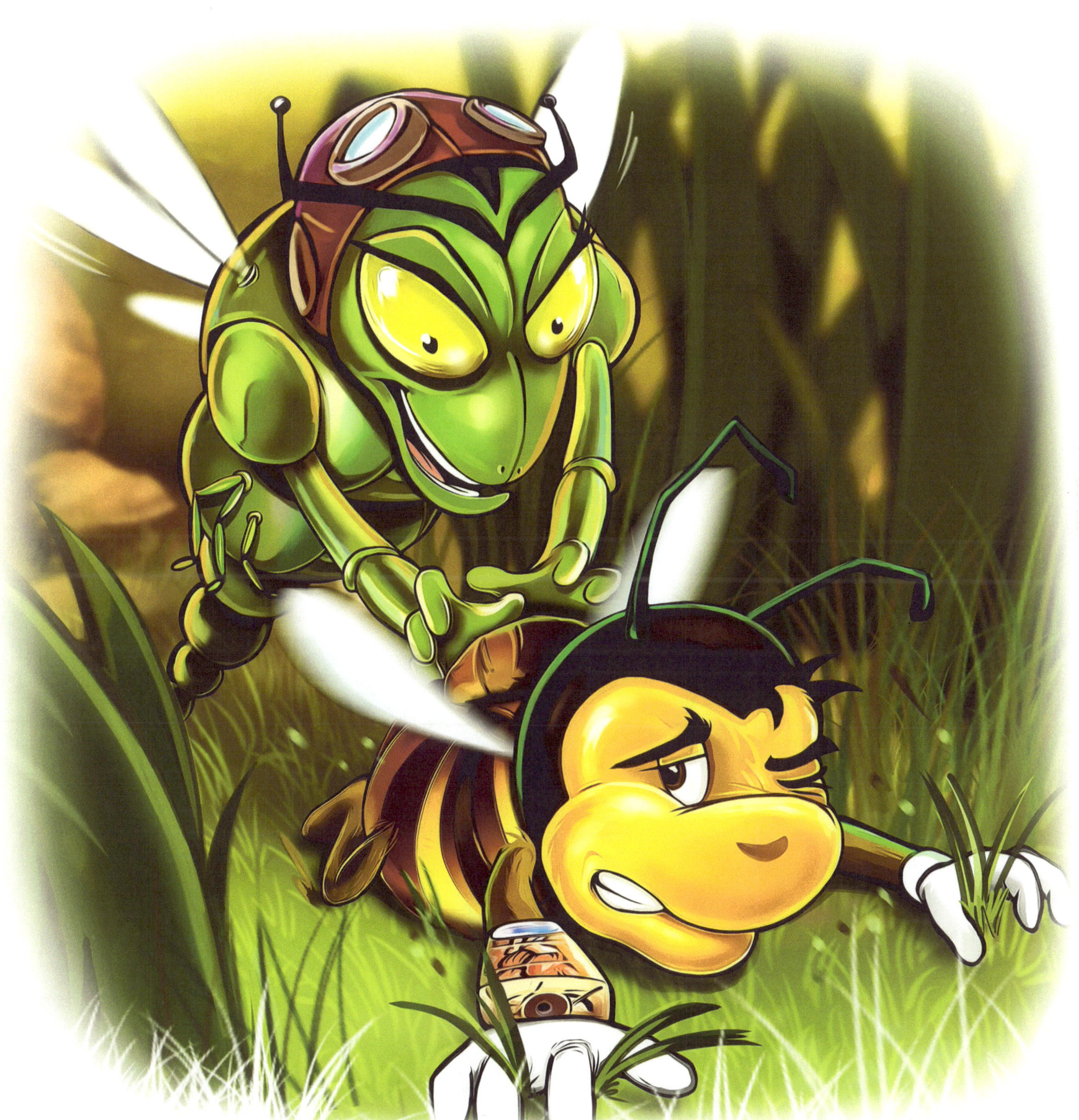

Suddenly, Jayce heard a loud "Splat!"
With one loud jerk, the dragonfly was slurped into the mouth of Sammy the Frog.
"Dragonflies are yummy to my tummy!"
Sammy gulped while licking his lips.

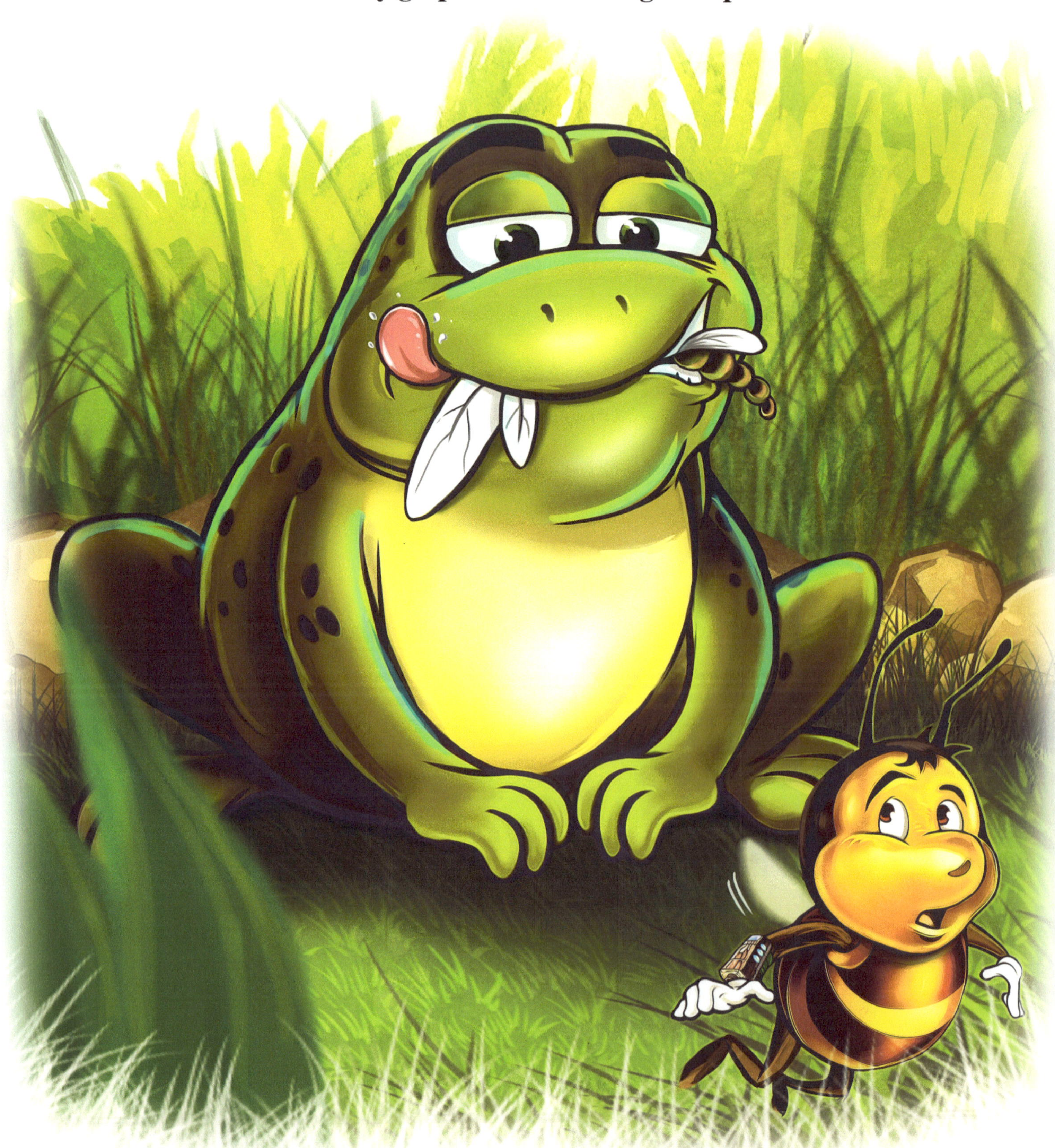

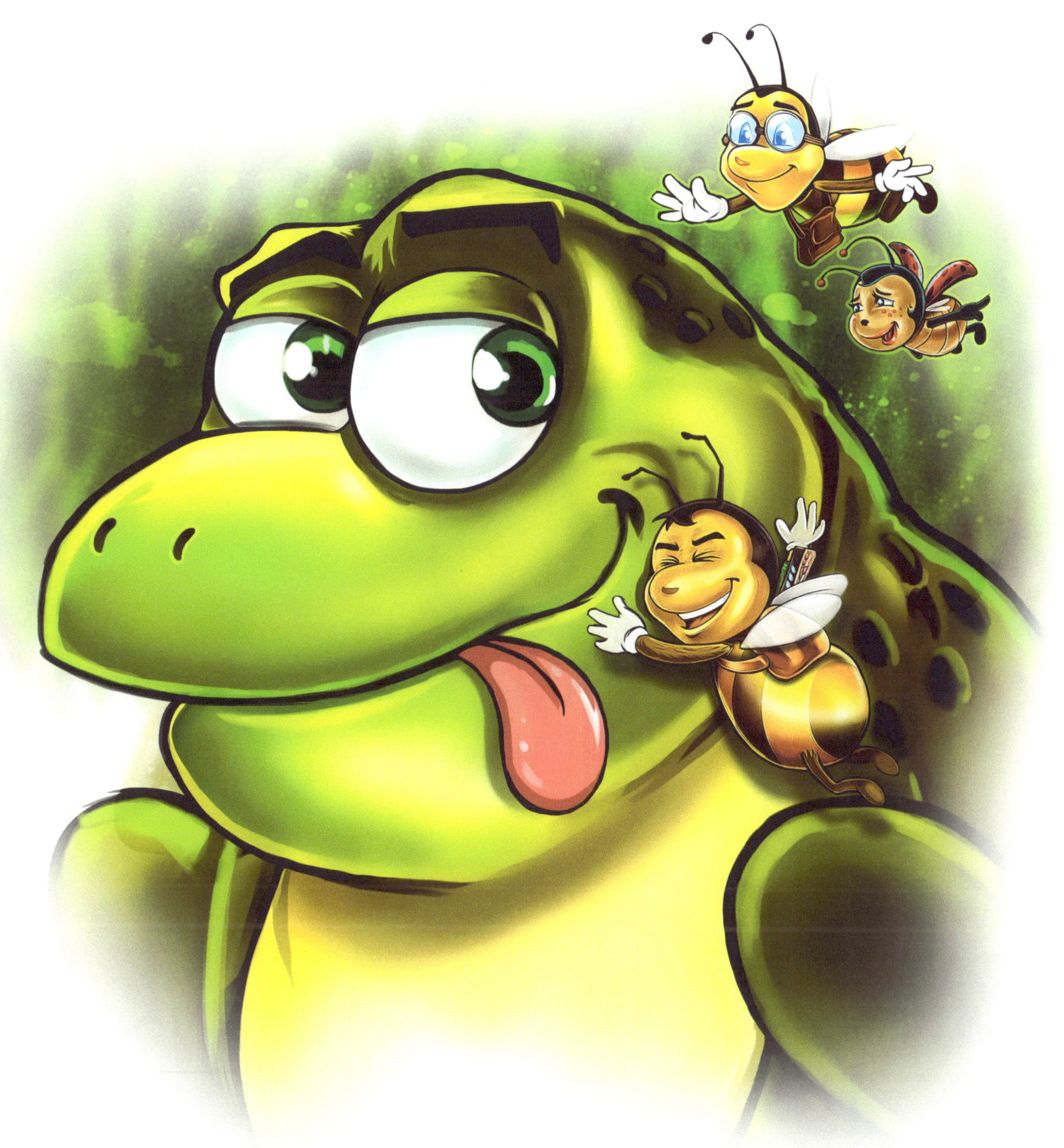

“Thank you!” Jayce said with a sigh of relief.
“You’re welcome. When I saw dragonflies chasing you, I figured I could help.” Sammy replied.
Jayce embraced Sammy with a big hug. When Lilly and Dex arrived, they were happy to see that Jayce was safe and sound.

"Earlier today you guys were happy to help me cross the pond, so I'm glad I was able to repay the favor," Sammy explained.
"When you're kind to others, it comes back around,"
Dex added with a smile.
The group said a final good-bye and Sammy hopped away.

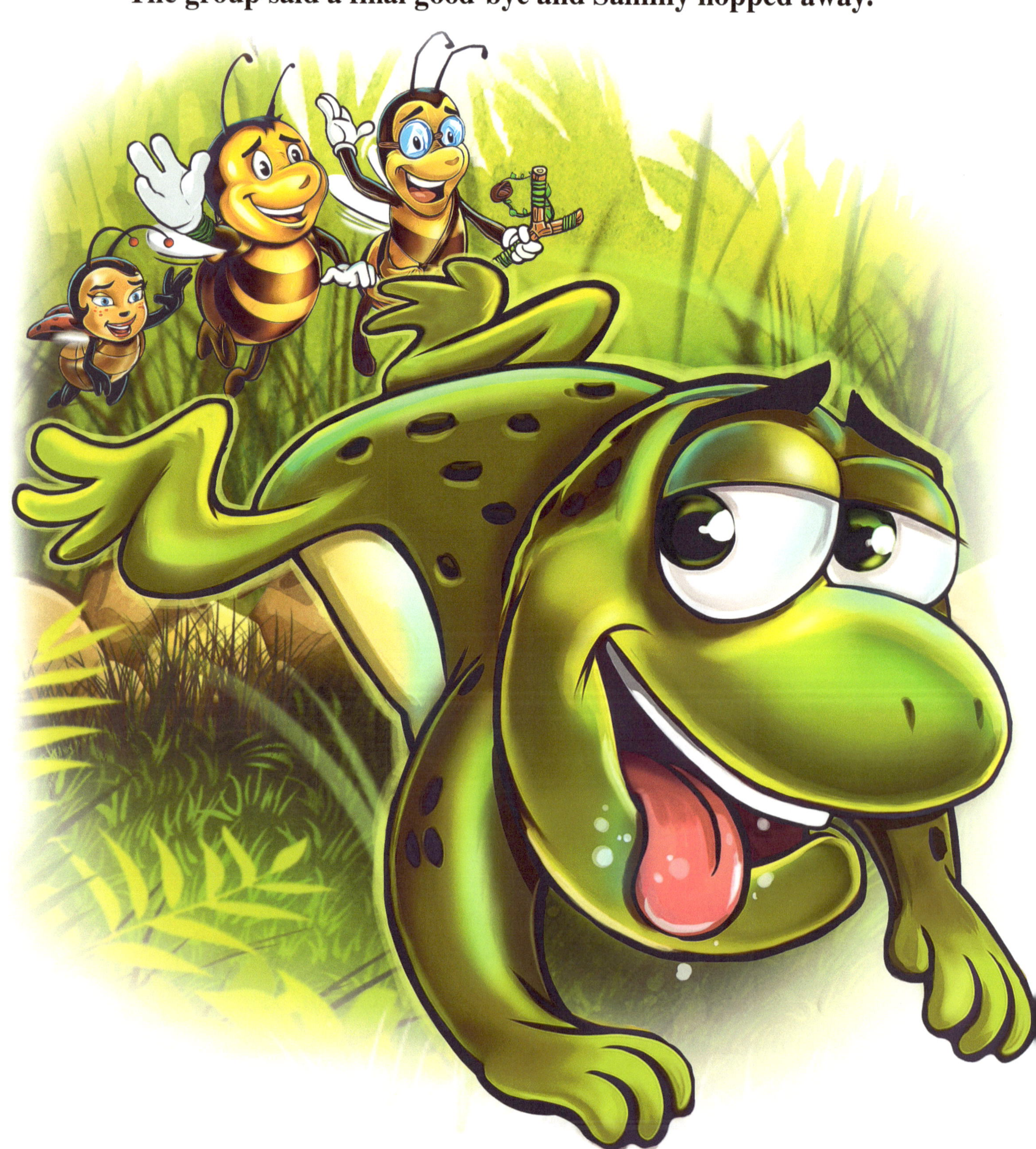

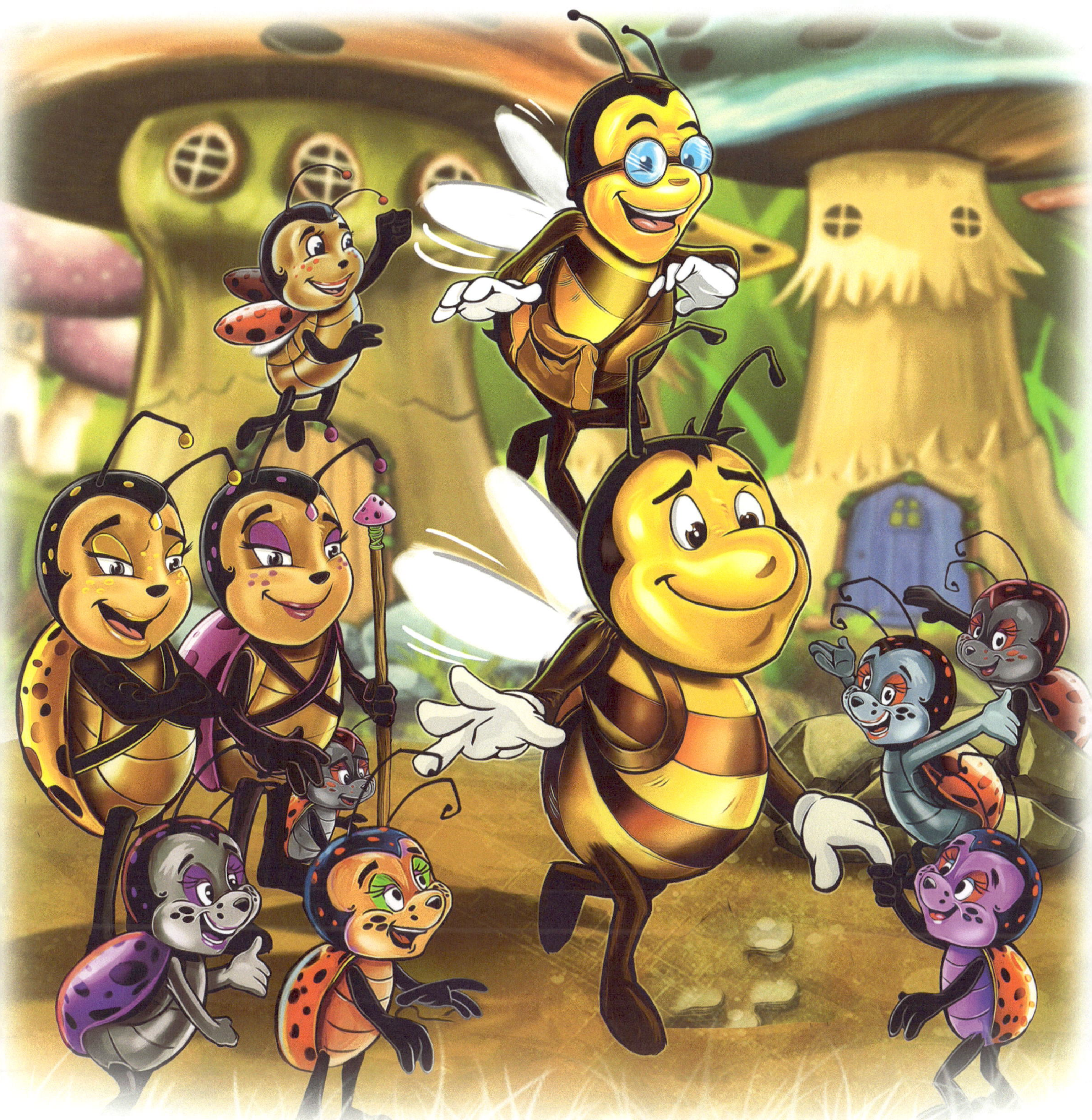

The three friends flew back to the Polka-Dot Village and stood before the ladybug elders. "We were wrong about you two," said Lady Loren. "Today, your bravery has made it crystal clear that you are indeed noble friends of the Polka-Dot Village!" All the ladybugs cheered happily while greeting their new bee friends.

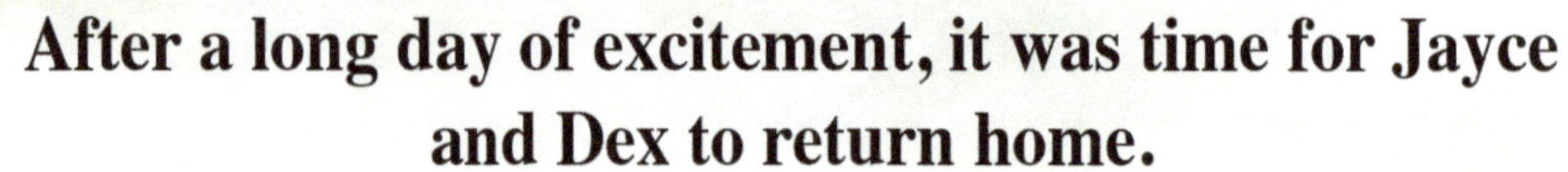

After a long day of excitement, it was time for Jayce and Dex to return home.
As they began to fly away, Jayce looked back and shouted, "We'll see you soon Lilly."
She smiled and waved good-bye until her friends vanished from her view.

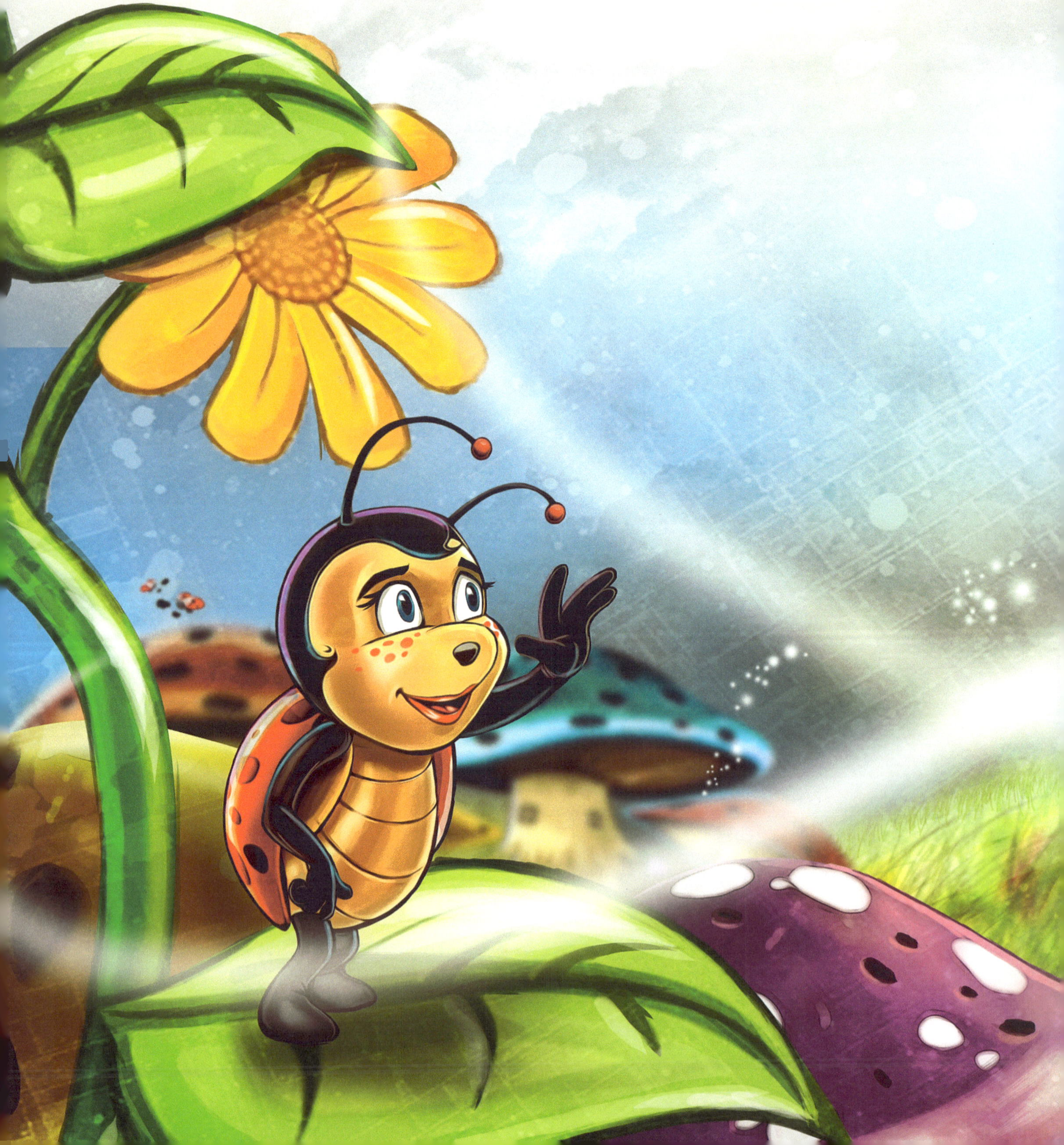

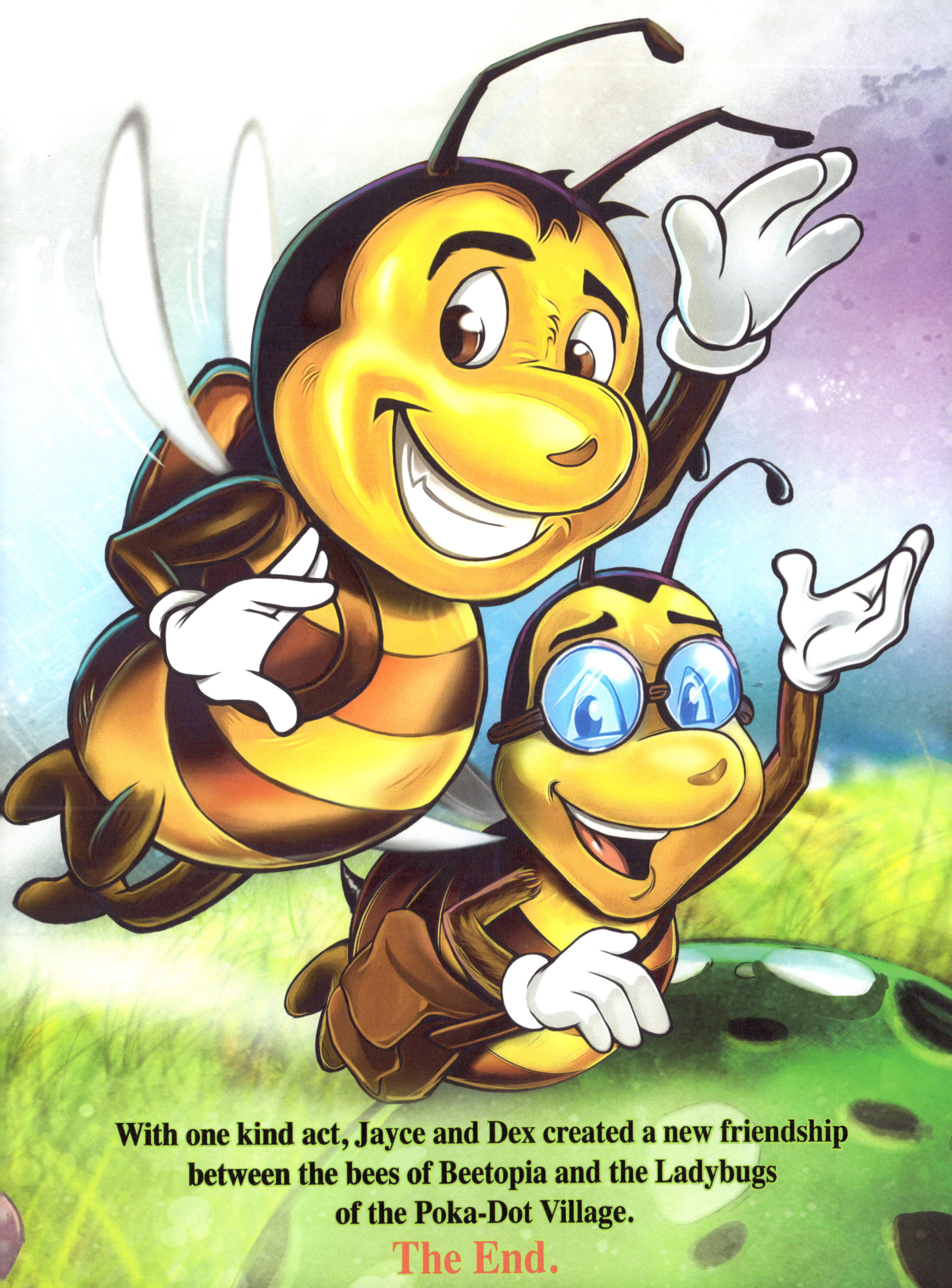

With one kind act, Jayce and Dex created a new friendship between the bees of Beetopia and the Ladybugs of the Poka-Dot Village.

The End.

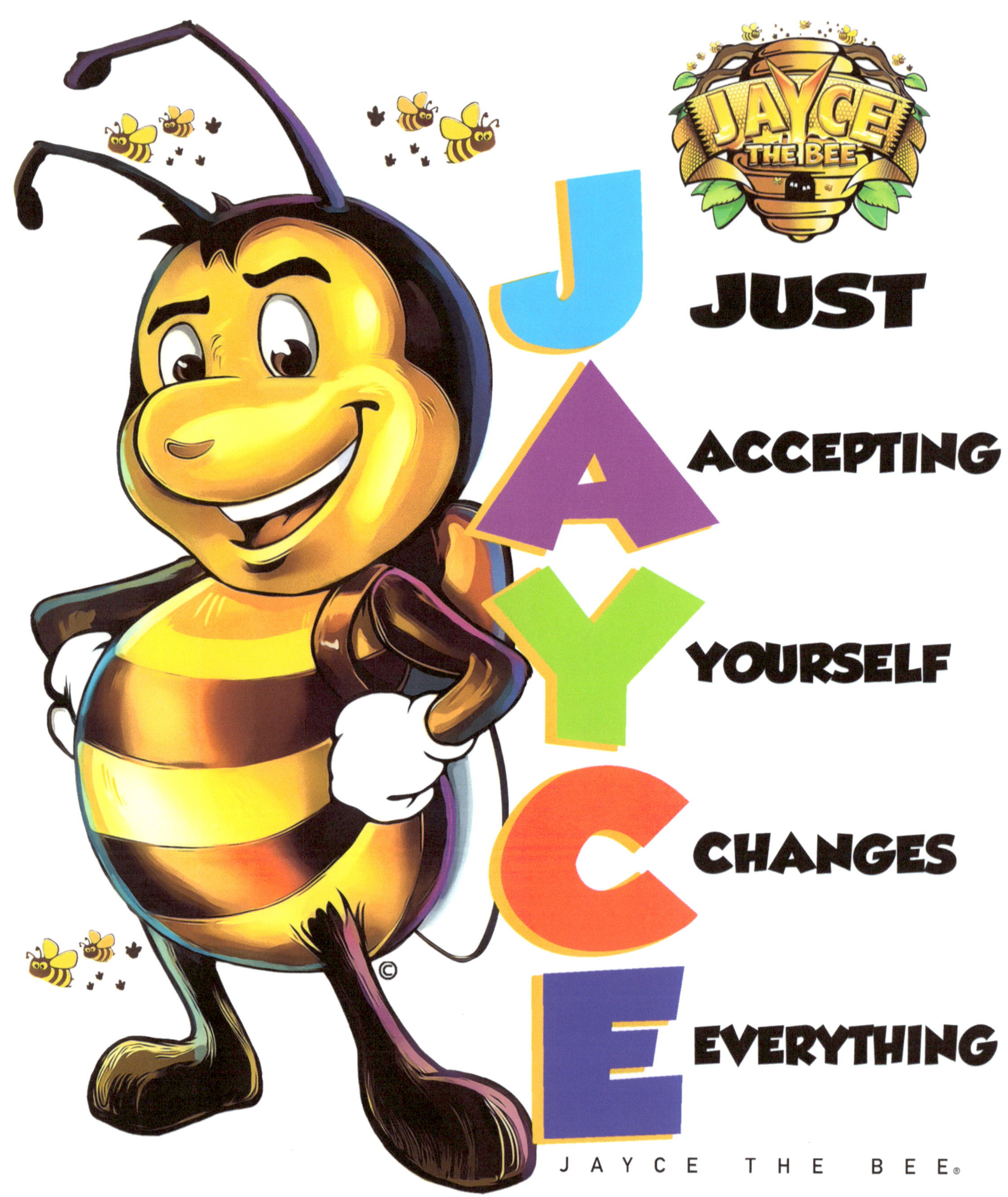
JAYCE THE BEE
J JUST
A ACCEPTING
Y YOURSELF
C CHANGES
E EVERYTHING
©
JAYCE THE BEE®

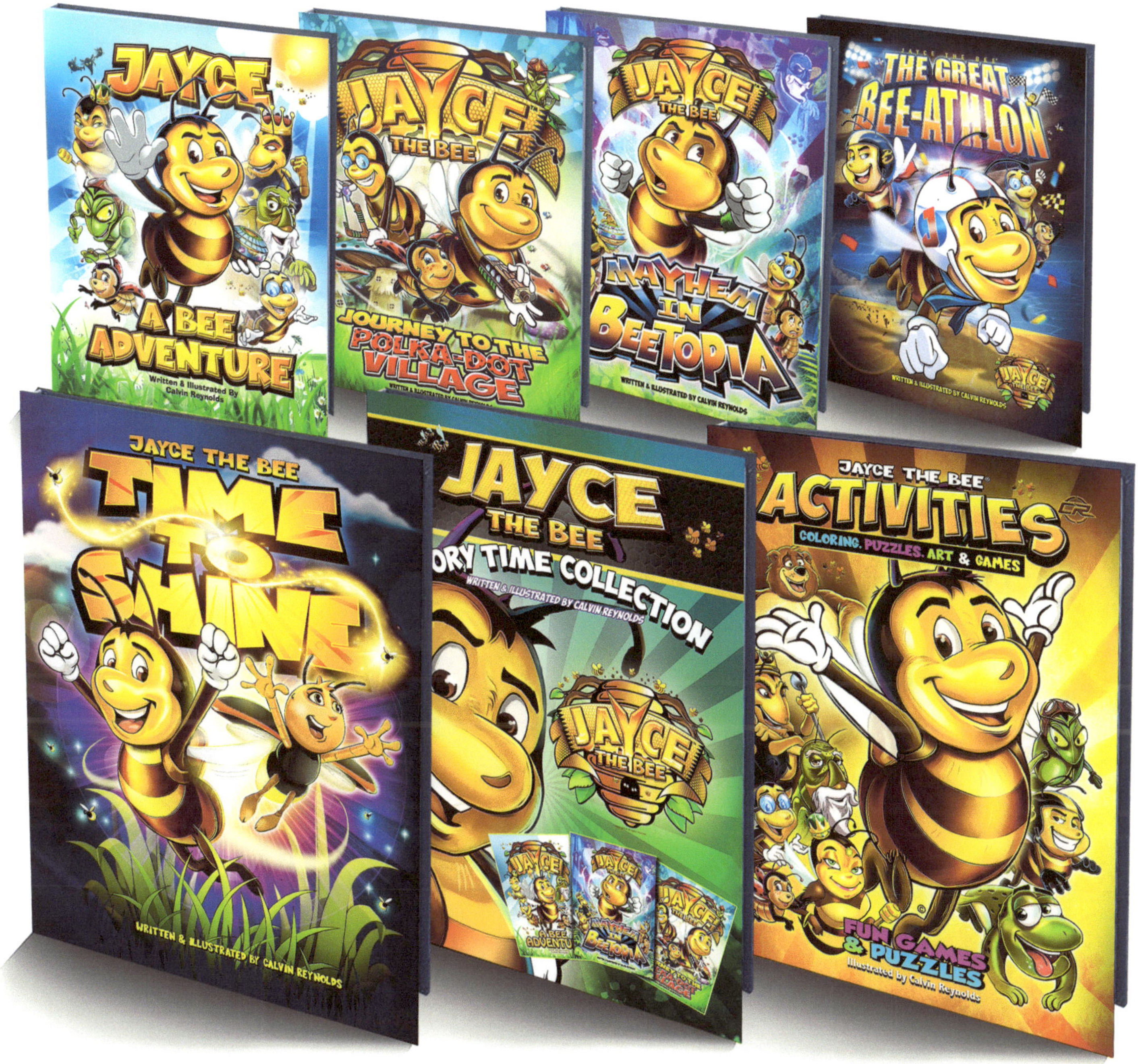

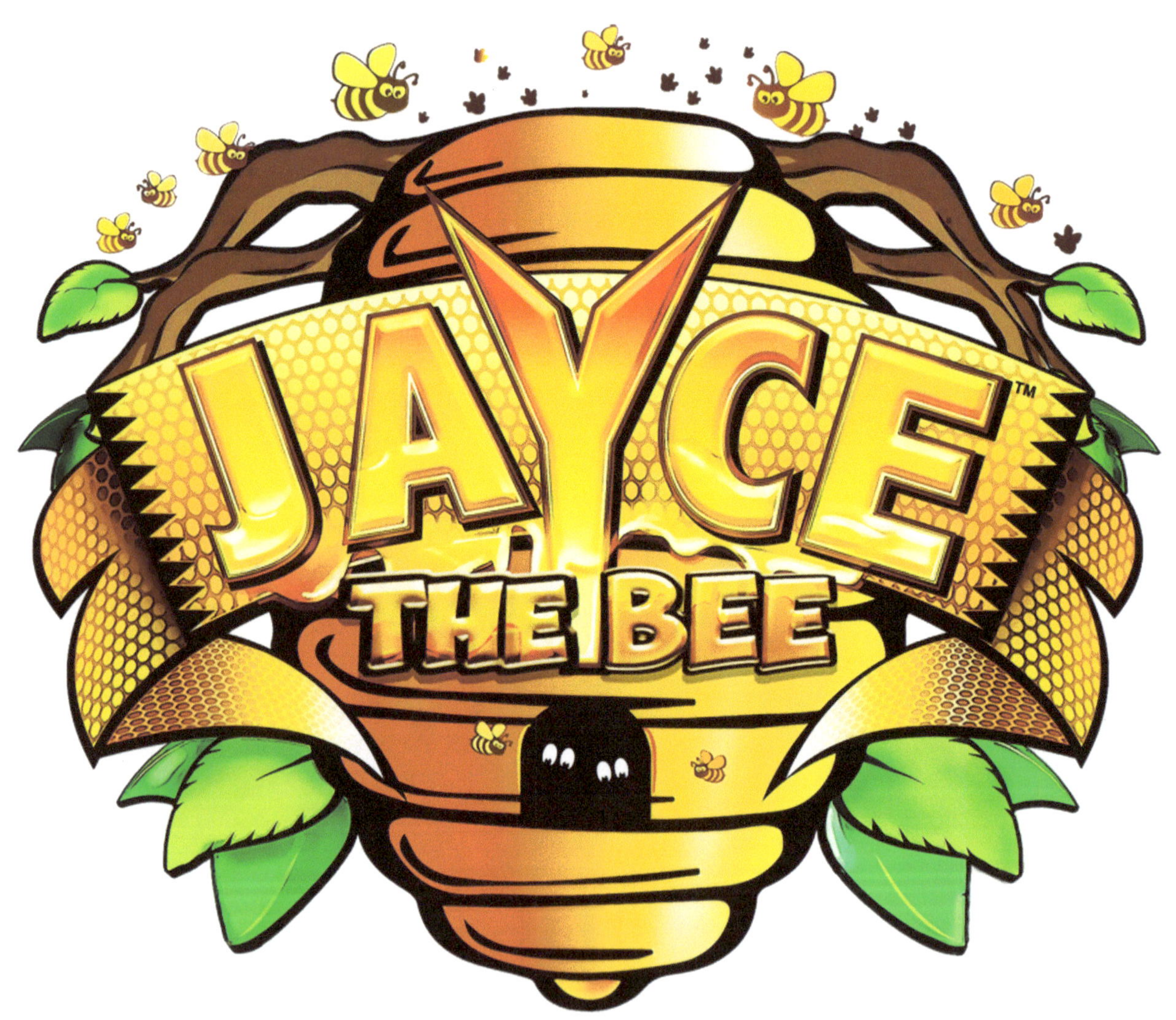
JAYCE™
THE BEE

www.ingramcontent.com/pod-product-compliance
Lightning Source LLC
LaVergne TN
LVHW070159110826
845147LV00002B/446

9780998663005